PLANTS
AND
PLANT LIFE

VOLUME 5
Plants Used by People

MICHAEL ALLABY

GROLIER
EDUCATIONAL

About this Set

PLANTS AND PLANT LIFE *is a ten-volume set that describes the world of plants in all its facets. Volume by volume, you will be introduced to the many different aspects of plant life.*

The first three volumes (1: Roots, Stems, and Leaves, 2: Flowers and Fruits, and 3: Life Processes) explain the basic structure, reproductive methods, and processes of life in flowering plants.

Volume 4 (Plant Ecology) explores the place of plants in the living community of life on Earth, while Volume 5 (Plants Used by People) presents the literally hundreds of plants that have been exploited by people for food, clothing, building, and many other uses.

The final five volumes (6: Algae and Fungi, 7: Mosses and Ferns, 8: Conifers, 9: Flowering Plants—The Monocotyledons, and 10: Flowering Plants—The Dicotyledons) lead the reader on a journey of discovery through the main groups of life that are usually classed as plants. In these volumes the typical and characteristic features of each group and its components are clearly outlined.

Though each volume deals with a distinct aspect of plant life, many of them are interrelated. To help you understand these links, every entry has enlightening cross-references to other entries and volumes. Throughout the set you will also find special short boxed features— entitled "Protecting Our World"—that focus on particular stories of environmental concern.

The whole set is liberally illustrated with diagrams explaining plant processes and structures, with depictions of typical plants and maps showing global distribution. In addition, hundreds of photographs bring the world of plants vividly to life. At the end of every volume there is a useful glossary explaining the technical terms that are used in the text, an index to all the volumes in the set, and finally, a list of other sources of reference (both books and websites). All the plants mentioned in the volume are listed alphabetically by common name, with their scientific names alongside.

Contents

Published 2001 by Grolier Educational, Danbury, CT 06816

This edition published exclusively for the school and library market

Planned and produced by Andromeda Oxford Limited, 11–13 The Vineyard, Abingdon, Oxon OX14 3PX, UK www.andromeda.co.uk

Copyright © Andromeda Oxford Limited 2001

Project Director: *Graham Bateman*
Editorial Manager: *Peter Lewis*
Art Editors and Designers: *Martin Anderson, Chris Munday, Steve McCurdy*
Editors: *Penelope Isaac, Eleanor Stillwell*
Cartography: *Richard Watts, Tim Williams*
Editorial Assistant: *Marian Dreier*
Picture Manager: *Claire Turner*
Production: *Clive Sparling*
Index: *Ann Barrett*

Originated and printed in Hong Kong

Library of Congress Cataloging-in-Publication Data

Plants and plant life.
    p.   cm.
    Includes bibliographical references.
    Contents: v.1. Roots, stems, and leaves -- v. 2. Flowers and fruits -- v. 3. Life processes -- v. 4. Plant ecology -- v. 5. Plants used by people -- v. 6. Algae and fungi -- v. 7. Mosses and ferns -- v. 8. Conifers -- v. 9. Flowering plants--the Monocotyledons -- v. 10. Flowering plants--the Dicotyledons.
    ISBN 0-7172-9510-9 (set : alk. paper) -- ISBN 0-7172-9515-X (vol. 5)
    1. Plants--Juvenile literature. 2. Botany--Juvenile literature. [1.Plants--Encyclopedias. 2. Botany--Encyclopedias.] 1. Grolier Educational Corporation.

QK49 .P54 2000
580--dc21
                                99-056140

Set ISBN 0–7172–9510–9

Volume 5 ISBN 0–7172–9515–X

Domestication

ABOUT 10,000 YEARS AGO, in the countries now known as Syria, northern Iraq, and southern Turkey people began to change the way they lived. Until this time they had gathered wild plants to obtain their edible seeds. Now they began to grow the plants themselves. This was the start of a process called domestication.

◀ An Egyptian painting shows workers using sickles to harvest wheat about 5,000 years ago.

ancestors of the early crops, of emmer and einkorn wheat, and of barley, still grow naturally in parts of the Middle East.

The Beginning of Farming

As the cultivation of crops spread into Europe, unwanted seeds—including oats and rye—also spread, having been mixed with the grain for sowing. Oats and rye also produced edible seeds and could grow in areas too cold and wet for wheat and barley, so they were selected for cultivation as well. This allowed farming to expand still further.

Agriculture was invented. Farming made it possible to produce bigger quantities of better-quality food; with more to eat, fewer people died from hunger and malnutrition. Populations increased in size and then had to feed themselves by farming because wild plants could no longer provide enough food.

Domestication involved bringing wild crops under control so that they could be cultivated. The change happened gradually, as the knowledge of how to grow crops for food spread, and more communities adopted the methods. This also meant a change from a nomadic, wandering lifestyle. Instead of moving around searching for food in the wild, people could now grow it where they lived. From every crop they harvested, some grain was set aside to use as seed stock for the next year, while the rest was eaten.

At first people grew wheat and barley. They are grasses; but unlike many grass species, they are annuals: new plants grow from seed each year. The plants produce many seeds, and when cooked, the seeds are edible. They can be boiled, or ground to make flour and then baked. The

Domestication in Other Parts of the World

In addition to cereals Middle Eastern farmers began cultivating other plants. They grew peas, chickpeas, lentils, and broad beans. They also grew flax; from it they obtained oil, as well as a fiber that they made into linen cloth. Over the next few thousand years agriculture began in other parts of the world. People far from the Middle East also developed the knowledge of how to increase their food supplies by cultivating edible plants instead of gathering food from the wild.

We know that by about 9,000 years ago people were growing rice in northern and central China and in Southeast Asia. Foxtail millet, another grass with edible seeds, was cultivated in northern China. By 5,000 years ago both rice and sorghum (a relative of millet) were being grown in the Sudan and along the southern edge of the Sahara Desert.

There were also farmers in Central and South America. In Mexico 8,000 years ago they were growing teosinte, the wild ancestor of corn (maize). Along with corn Mexican farmers grew

peppers (capsicums), runner beans, kidney beans, tepary beans, and squash.

Pumpkins, a type of squash, were first cultivated in South America, and 4,000 years ago they were grown in eastern North America, as were sunflowers. Much later, perhaps about 2,000 years ago, potatoes were cultivated farther south in the Andes.

▼ Plants were domesticated in many different parts of the world. Later they were grown wherever the soil and climate were suitable.

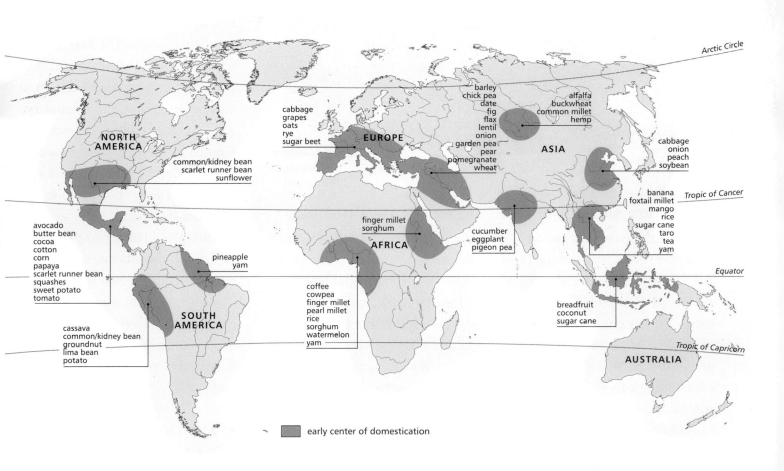

early center of domestication

See Also | SEEDS 2 28 | CEREALS 5 12 | GRASS FAMILY 9 12 ◉

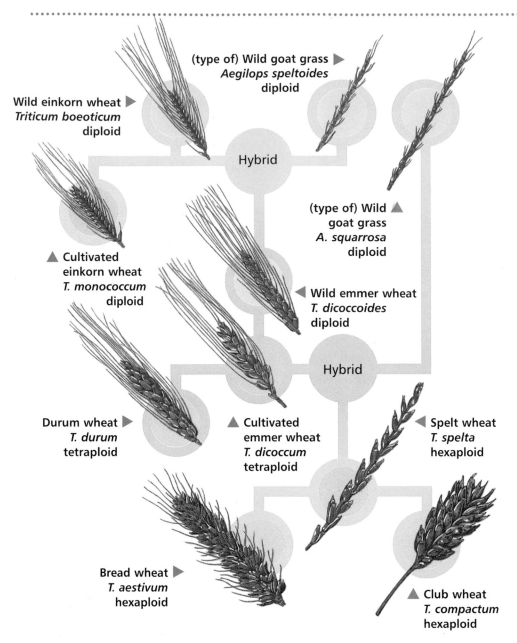

Wild einkorn wheat ▶
Triticum boeoticum
diploid

(type of) Wild goat grass ▶
Aegilops speltoides
diploid

Hybrid

(type of) Wild ▲
goat grass
A. squarrosa
diploid

▲ Cultivated
einkorn wheat
T. monococcum
diploid

◀ Wild emmer wheat
T. dicoccoides
diploid

Hybrid

Durum wheat ▶
T. durum
tetraploid

▲ Cultivated
emmer wheat
T. dicoccum
tetraploid

◀ Spelt wheat
T. spelta
hexaploid

Bread wheat ▶
T. aestivum
hexaploid

◀ Club wheat
T. compactum
hexaploid

MODERN WHEAT

◀ Modern wheat is descended from wild einkorn wheat, wild emmer wheat, and goat grass. In the course of its cultivation it has increased the number of its chromosomes from two sets (diploid) to four sets (tetraploid) to six sets (hexaploid) in the varieties grown today.

Key
⬤ plants that shed their seed
⬤ plants that retain seed
⬤ plants from which seed must be removed by threshing

Retaining seeds in the ear is a characteristic that plants inherit. It is transmitted in the seeds from one generation to the next. By selecting seeds only from plants that did not shed their seeds, farmers encouraged the characteristic to become more widespread. Gradually, this altered the genetic composition of the cultivated plants, and they became quite different from their wild ancestors. All cultivated plants have been altered genetically as a result of being grown from seeds that were selected by farmers from individuals with particular qualities, such as large size, good flavor, attractive appearance, or high yield.

▶ **Wheat harvest in Oregon. A trailer filled with grain.**

Cultivation Alters Plants

When early farmers began to grow the plants that supplied food for their communities, they chose their seed with care. Annual grasses, for example, shed their seeds as soon as they are ripe. This gives the seeds the best chance of establishing new plants, but it also means they are difficult to harvest.

Cultivated grasses were grown from plants that did not shed their seeds, and some of those chosen plants provided the seeds that were planted to produce the next crop. Farmers deliberately selected grasses that did not shed their seeds, and eventually the cultivated varieties lost their ability to do so. Wheat, barley, oats, and rye that are grown on modern farms have to be threshed—by hand or, more usually, by machine—to remove the seeds from the ears.

Fruit Crops

MANY PLANTS PRODUCE SEEDS that are enclosed in tempting, fleshy, sweet fruits. As the seeds mature and the fruit ripens, the amount of sugar in the fruit increases. In the wild animals eat the energy-rich fruit and then scatter the seed away from the parent plant. Today we benefit from this fruitful harvest.

If the seeds of the plants are big, like the stone from a peach, an animal discards them. If they are small, like the seeds of strawberries, an animal eats them but does not digest them. They pass through its body unchanged and are discarded in the feces.

To this day, even in advanced industrial countries like the United States, people enjoy gathering wild berries. However, the fruit in our stores has been grown from cultivated varieties. In some cases they are very different from their wild ancestors.

Apples, Pears, and Plums

Apples are descended from the wild crab apple, the fruit of a tree that grows naturally in much of southeastern Europe and southwestern Asia. Crab apples are very small, and even when ripe, they are hard and taste sour. Nevertheless, they featured in the diet of the earliest Europeans and were being cultivated at least 3,000 years ago.

The Romans planted apple trees throughout much of Europe, and the first settlers from Europe took them to America. Within a short time there were large orchards in eastern America, and by the middle of the 18th century apples were being exported to Britain from Virginia. In the early 19th century John Chapman (1774–1845) planted so many apple trees in Indiana and Ohio that he earned the nickname "Johnny Appleseed."

▶ Pictured are some of the many fruits that are descended from wild ancestors that grow naturally in temperate climates.

Pears are closely related to apples and originated in the same part of the world. Like apples, they have been much improved by cultivation. Wild pears are small, hard, and have little flavor. Pears were being grown in Greece

TEMPERATE FRUITS

Common name	Scientific name	Common name	Scientific name
1 Black currant	Ribes nigrum	14 Gage	Prunus institia
2 Red currant	Ribes rubrum	15 Medlar	Mespilus germanica
3 Bilberry	Vaccinium myrtillus	16 Quince	Cydonia vulgaris
4 Blueberry	Vaccinium corymbosum	17 Apricot	Prunus armeniaca
		18 Peach	Prunus persica
5 Sweet cherry	Prunus avium	19 Apple	Malus pumila
6 Cranberry	Vaccinium oxycoccus	20 Pear	Pyrus communis
7 Mulberry	Morus nigra	Blackberry	Rubus fruticosa
8 Gooseberry	Ribes uva-crispa	Grape	Vitis vinifera
9 Raspberry	Rubus idaeus	Grapefruit	Citrus paradisi
10 Plum	Prunus domestica	Lemon	Citrus limon
11 Strawberry	Fragaria x ananassa	Lime	Citrus aurantifolia
12 Fig	Ficus carica	Loganberry	Rubus loganobaccus
13 Damson	Prunus institia	Sweet orange	Citrus sinensis

3,000 years ago, and by 2,000 years ago improved varieties were being cultivated. European settlers took them to North America.

If wild apples and wild pears are unappetizing, the European wild plum, or sloe, is inedible. The fruit is small, very hard, and the flesh is very acid. It is from this unpromising start, together with the cherry plum (a species from western Asia), that we derive damsons, gages, prunes, and plums. Plums grown in warmer climates are descended from a different species, the Japanese plum. Other species grow naturally in North America and were eaten by Native Americans, but most cultivated American plums are now descended from the European varieties.

Peaches, nectarines, and apricots are close relatives of plums. They were first cultivated in China, possibly about 3,000 years ago. From there they were introduced throughout southwestern Asia and the Mediterranean region. Modern varieties are little different from those that were grown thousands of years ago.

Citrus Fruits

Citrus fruits also originated in China, as well as southeastern Asia and, in the case of the lime, in India. They have been cultivated since ancient times. Knowledge of how to grow them spread from China and India to East Africa, and from there to the lands bordering the eastern Mediterranean. The most familiar

▲ Strawberries must be picked by hand. Those shown are being gathered in California

member of the group, the sweet orange, was being grown in Italy by the 1st century A.D.

Christopher Columbus introduced oranges to America. The seeds—obtained in the Canary Isles—were planted in 1493, during his second expedition, at the settlement he established on the island of Hispaniola.

There are many species of citrus fruits. All of them have juice containing both sugars and acids. In some, such as the sweet orange and tangerine, sugars predominate. Others, such as the lemon and lime, are more acid. The grapefruit originated in the West Indies, either from a mutation of the pomelo or as a cross between a pomelo and a sweet

TROPICAL FRUITS

Common name	Scientific name	Common name	Scientific name
1 Pineapple	Ananas comosus	13 Guava	Psidium guajava
2 Durian	Durio zibethinus	14 Sapodilla	Manikara zapota
3 Mango	Mangifera indica	15 Passion fruit	Passiflora edulis
4 Papaw	Carica papaya	16 Loquat	Eriobotrya japonica
5 Soursop	Artocarpus muricata	17 Cape gooseberry	Physalis peruviana
6 Persimmon	Diospyros kaki	18 Rambutan	Nephelium lappaceum
7 Mangosteen	Garcinia mangostana		
8 Pomegranate	Punica granatum	Avocado	Persea americana
9 Litchi	Litchi chinensis	Breadfruit	Artocarpus altilis
10 Akee	Blighia sapida	Date	Phoenix dactylifera
11 Cherimoya	Annona cherimola	Jack fruit	Artocarpus heterophyllus
12 Banana	Musa acuminata		
		Sweetsop	Annona squamosa

orange. It was recognized as a species in 1830 and was first cultivated in about 1880, in Florida.

Many tropical fruits, such as the durian of Asia and the akee of West Africa, are eaten mainly in the countries where they are grown. Others, such as the banana and pineapple, are major exports for the countries that grow them. Yet others, including the litchi, mango, persimmon, and loquat, all from Asia, are becoming increasingly popular in Europe and America.

▶ **Many fruits grow only in tropical climates. Some are familiar favorites, like the pineapple and banana, but others, such as the durian and akee, are eaten mainly in the countries where they grow.**

See Also | *BANANA FAMILY* **9** *40* | *CITRUS FRUIT FAMILY* **10** *36* | *SUNFLOWER FAMILY* **10** *46* 👁

Cereals

OF ALL THE FOOD CROPS THAT FARMERS GROW, wheat and rice are by far the most important. They are cereals—a word derived from Ceres, the Roman goddess of agriculture—and they provide the staple foods that form the basis of the diet of most people. Every year, in the world as a whole farmers produce about 650 million tons of wheat and more than 400 million tons of rice.

Cereals are very versatile foods. Grains can be used whole or ground into a flour. Coarsely ground wheat grains are called semolina. Roasted or boiled, or mixed with a little water and oil, they make couscous, a North African dish. Whole grains that have been boiled, dried, and crushed are known as bulgur wheat, which can be used in salads and stuffings.

Bread, Cakes, and Pasta

Most wheat is ground finely to make flour, which is used to make bread, pasta, cakes, and pastries.

Wheat grains contain more of the protein gluten than those of other cereal crops, and varieties of wheat can be grouped according to their gluten content. When wet, gluten becomes elastic and makes a good dough. Wheat with a high gluten content is called hard. It is used to make bread. Rye and barley can also be used to make bread. Soft wheat, with less gluten, is used to make cakes.

▼ All cereals are grasses. The most important for food are wheat, rice, corn, millet, sorghum, oats, rye, and barley.

CEREALS

Common name	Scientific name
1 Bread wheat	Triticum aestivum
2 Durum wheat	Triticum durum
3 Rye	Secale cereale
4 Oats	Avena sativa
5 Barley (six-rowed)	Hordeum vulgare
6 Corn (maize)	Zea mays
7 Rice	Oryza sativa
8 Sorghum	Sorghum vulgare
9 Finger millet	Eleusine coracana
10 Little millet	Panicum miliare
11 Foxtail millet	Setaria italica
Barley (two-rowed)	Hordeum distichon
Japanese millet	Echinochloa frumentacea
Spelt wheat	Triticum spelta
Wild rice	Zizania aquatica

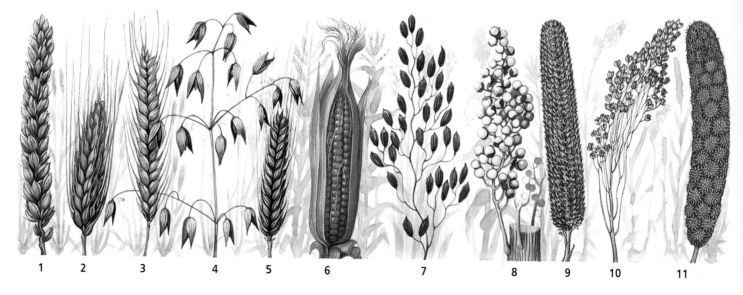

1   2   3   4   5   6   7   8   9   10   11

Durum is the hardest wheat of all. It is used to make pasta. Pasta was invented in China, as noodles, which is where European travelers learned of it.

Upland Rice and Paddy Rice

Most rice is grown in Asia, where it has been a staple food for thousands of years. It can be grown in rows on dry land, like wheat, in hilly areas. Rice grown in this way is known as upland rice. Less than one-fifth of the world's rice is grown in this way, however, since there is another method that yields much larger crops.

Rice seeds are sown in dry soil. As soon as they sprout, seedlings are transplanted into fields that have been plowed and then flooded, the young plants being placed into the mud below the water. When the grains ripen, the water is drained from the flooded fields—called paddies—so the ground is dry for harvesting.

Corn, Millet, and Sorghum

Corn (maize) is grown over a large area of the United States and is an important cereal crop in parts of the world with long summers. In Africa it is known

▲ **Wheat being harvested in North America, where this cultivated grass has replaced the natural prairie grasses over a large area.**

as "mealies." Corn originated in Central America, where it was cultivated by Native Americans. Christopher Columbus introduced it to Europe.

Millet and sorghum are usually eaten as a porridge made by cooking the pounded grain in water. They are important cereal crops in Africa, parts of Europe, and Asia.

See Also | *DOMESTICATION 5 4* | *GRASS FAMILY 9 12* ◉

Nuts

AS THEY WALKED THROUGH THE FOREST searching for food, our ancestors would have looked out for trees bearing edible nuts. They would have enjoyed the taste and texture of such easily digestible foods, and would have benefited from their highly nutritious kernels. They are "energy foods," rich in fats and protein.

Whole nuts provide a tasty snack. They can also be ground into a flour and used in many ways. Unfortunately, some people have an allergy to nuts and cannot eat them.

Most of the nuts we buy now are grown on commercial plantations, often far from the regions where they occur naturally. For example, the Romans introduced the sweet chestnut (originally from southern Europe) to many parts of Europe. Almonds are used to make marzipan, a paste used in confectionery. They originated in the Near East, but are now grown in California, southern Australia, and South Africa.

Coconuts and Chestnuts

The coconut palm tree is one of the most useful plants in the world. Little of it goes to waste. The coconut is the "stone" inside a fruit that has a thick, fibrous husk. Contained inside a very tough shell is a sweet, refreshing coconut "milk." As the fruit ripens, most of the liquid is absorbed into the white "meat" of the nut. It can be eaten directly or dried and pressed to make copra, from which oil can be harvested. The fibers of the outer husk are used to make coir, from which coconut matting and ropes are made. The palm tree provides timber for building and leaves for thatching.

Roasted chestnuts are a winter favorite. The raw nut can be ground to a flour that is used in soups, stuffings, and other foods or cooked and glazed with sugar syrup to make the French delicacy marron glacé. The water chestnut, although similar, is not related to the chesnut—nor is it related to the Chinese water chestnut, used in Chinese dishes.

Walnuts, Pecans, and Pistachios

Walnuts grow naturally from southeastern Europe to China, but for centuries they have been cultivated farther north. France is the major commercial producer,

NUTS

Common name	Scientific name	Common name	Scientific name
1 Pecan	*Carya illinoinensis*	14 Betel nut	*Areca catechu*
2 Black walnut	*Juglans nigra*	15 Kola nut	*Cola nitida*
3 Sweet chestnut	*Castanea sativa*	16 Macadamia nut (smooth shell)	*Macadamia integrifolia*
4 Hazelnut	*Corylus avellana*	Macadamia nut (rough shell)	*Macadamia tetraphylla*
5 Walnut	*Juglans regia*	17 Brazil nut	*Bertholletia excelsa*
6 Water chestnut	*Trapa natans*		
7 Giant filbert	*Corylus maxima*	Chinese water chestnut	*Eleocharis tuberosa*
8 Butternut	*Juglans cinerea*		
9 Cashew nut	*Anacardium occidentale*	Groundnut (peanut) (see also Vegetables; Oil crops)	*Arachis hypogaea*
10 Almond	*Prunus amygdalus*		
11 Pistachio	*Pistacia vera*	Moreton Bay chestnut	*Catanospermum australe*
12 Coconut	*Cocos nucifera*		
13 Pine nut	*Pinus pinea*		

but the nuts are also grown elsewhere. The black walnut and the butternut (or white walnut), both close relatives of the Eurasian walnut, are natives of North America. Black walnut shells are too thick to be broken by normal nutcrackers, although varieties have been bred with thinner shells. They are used mainly in confectionery and ice cream.

Pecans are also related to walnuts. They are eaten raw and used in cakes, ice cream, and confectionery. Although they have long been appreciated in North America, Europeans have been introduced to them only recently.

Pistachios are another favorite, not least for their unusual green kernels. They are grown in the southern United States, but they came originally from Iran. They are cultivated from the Mediterranean region to Afghanistan.

Cashews and Brazil Nuts

The cashew, a native of the West Indies, is related to the pistachio. It grows in a curious way. A single nut is produced on the underside of a large fleshy fruit called an "apple" (because it looks like one). The apple is eaten locally, mainly as jelly. Cashews are now grown commercially in India and Africa.

Brazil nuts are harvested from trees in the forests of Brazil and Venezuela. Most are exported to the United States and Europe. A circle of 12–24 nuts forms in a woody, hard fruit. Each fruit weighs up to 4 pounds (1.8 kg) and must be broken open to obtain the nuts.

▼ Nuts have a kernel rich in oil and protein, enclosed in a shell. Many trees produce them in temperate regions and in the tropics.

See Also | *SEEDS* **2** *28* | *PLANTS & THE ECOSYSTEM* **4** *4* | *VEGETABLES* **5** *16* | *PALM FAMILY* **9** *30* ◉

Vegetables

ABOUT THE SAME TIME AS FARMERS started to cultivate cereals, they also began to domesticate the plants that we call vegetables. In particular they began to cultivate peas, beans, and lentils. Seeds of such plants are rich in protein, so they greatly improve a diet based on wheat, rice, or corn.

It is not only the seeds of plants that we eat as vegetables. We also eat many other parts of plants, including the fruit of some, and call all of them vegetables. We even eat the leaf stalks of one plant, rhubarb, but cooked as a dessert, so we treat it as though it were a fruit.

Onions

Onions were domesticated long ago; along with garlic they were eaten by workers building the pyramids of ancient Egypt. Like other vegetables, onions can be eaten raw, fried, boiled, stewed, or roasted. An important ingredient of many dishes, onions are also used in chutneys and pickles.

We eat many types of onions: shallot, scallion, and leek. The part that we eat is called a bulb. The garlic clove is called a bulbil. Garlic bulbils form in a densely packed group surrounded by layers of papery tissue. The group of cloves is called a bulb, although a true bulb is made up of the fleshy bases of leaves tightly wrapped around each other.

The origin of the onion is uncertain. It is possible it is descended from a wild ancestor that grew near the Dead Sea more than 5,000 years ago. Leeks have no living wild relatives, but are probably descended from a plant that grows in the regions around the Mediterranean.

Tomatoes

Botanically, the tomato is a berry because it is a fruit that contains many seeds. It has been bred from a relative of the potato that grows in South America. When it was first introduced to Italy in the 16th century, it was known as the *pomo d'oro* (golden apple) which indicates that it was probably a yellow variety. From Italy it was taken to France, where it was called the *pomme d'amour* (love apple). It was also known as the Peruvian apple in recognition of the country from which it came. In North America many people believed it to be toxic. Its genus is *Lycopersicon,* which means "wolf peach," implying that eating it may be dangerous!

Although the first tomatoes to reach Europe were yellow, the red varieties are more familiar. Many varieties have been bred for particular uses. Tomatoes are counted as vegetables rather than fruit because they are most commonly used in the main part of a meal, either alone or as an ingredient in a cooked dish.

Peppers and Globe Artichokes

Bell peppers, or capsicums, are fruits also classed as vegetables. Like tomatoes, they came originally from tropical America and the West Indies. Capsicums are berries containing many seeds. When ripe, the fruits are red, yellow, or brown, but they are often used when they are still green. The flesh is very rich in vitamin C. Large capsicums, known as sweet peppers, can be eaten raw, but the seeds are pungent. In parts of Europe some varieties are called paprika, and in Spain they are called pimientos.

Red peppers, or chilies, are smaller varieties, sometimes

counted as a species in their own right. Grown in the tropics, the ripe fruits are dried in the Sun. Cooks grate as much as they need to flavor their dishes, but each variety of chili varies in strength. Dried fruits are crushed to make cayenne pepper, and chilies are also used to make Tabasco sauce. (The sauce is named after Tabasco, a state in Mexico.)

Globe artichokes were grown by the ancient Greeks and Romans. The plant looks like a thistle with very large flowers. The flower bud is enclosed in fleshy scales, or bracts. After the whole bud is cooked, it is the base of the bracts that are eaten.

Stalks and Leaves

A relative of the globe artichoke, called the cardoon, is cultivated in southern Europe for its leaf stalks. They are blanched—partly cooked in boiling water—and then used like celery. A growing cardoon resembles a globe artichoke, but its leaves and bracts have more prickles. It is not grown commercially because the plants need a great deal of care

▲ Vegetables are grown commercially on a large scale. The bell peppers here have been picked in California and are being loaded into hoppers to be taken away for sorting and packing.

and work, but it was introduced to South America, where it became naturalized. It now grows throughout the pampas. Its flowers are used to curdle milk.

Celery is also grown for its edible leaf stalks. The plant grows wild in many parts of the world, usually near water. The cultivated

See Also | BULBS, CORMS, AND RHIZOMES **1** 34 | LILY FAMILY **9** 20 | POTATO FAMILY **10** 40 👁

1

2

3

4

5

6

7

8

9

10

11

12

13

14

VEGETABLES

◄ We eat the bulbs of onions, shallots, leeks, and garlic, the flower bracts of globe artichokes, the fruits of tomatoes, the stems of rhubarb and celery, the shoots of asparagus, the leaf bases of Florence fennel, and the leaves of spinach, lettuce, chicory, and chives.

plant is a variety of the wild one, not a separate species.

The origin of the rhubarb plant is obscure, but it may be descended from a wild plant that is found in parts of eastern Europe and northern Asia. Rhubarb leaves contain oxalic

TEMPERATE VEGETABLES

Common name	Scientific name
1 Chives	*Allium schoenoprasum*
2 Shallot	*Allium cepa* var. *aggregatum*
3 Onion	*Allium cepa*
4 Garlic	*Allium sativum*
5 Leek	*Allium porrum*
6 Tomato	*Lycopersicon esculentum*
7 Globe artichoke	*Cynara scolymus*
8 Rhubarb	*Rheum rhabarbarum*
9 Spinach	*Spinacia oleracea*
10 Lettuce	*Lactuca sativa*
11 Asparagus	*Asparagus officinalis*
12 Florence fennel	*Foeniculum vulgare* var. *azoricum*
13 Chicory	*Cichorium intybus*
14 Celery	*Apium graveolens*

acid and are toxic—people have died from eating them. The leaf stalks are harmless, however, and are cooked as a dessert or used as a flavoring.

Sea kale grows wild around the coasts of Europe. It was once quite widely cultivated, although it is seldom grown today. When blanched, the leaf stalks taste a bit like asparagus.

Asparagus, also native to Europe, has been cultivated for more than 2,000 years. The young shoot is cut when it is about 12 inches (30 cm) tall. It is usually poached before eating.

With other plants, such as spinach and lettuce, it is the leaves that are eaten. Spinach originally came from southwestern Asia. Spinach beet and chard (also called seakale beet) have edible leaves very like spinach. They are part of a subspecies of the beetroot and sugar-beet plant. It is known that the ancient Persians grew lettuces, and by Roman times there were several varieties. Endive and chicory have also been cultivated for thousands of years. Their leaves, when shaded from the light, are very pale in color and are eaten in salads. If the leaves are green, they are too bitter. Endive is one of the "bitter herbs" eaten before the ritual meal of the Jewish Passover.

See Also | *LEAVES 1 38* | *THE FLOWER 2 4* | *FRUITS 2 32* ◉

Varieties of Cabbage

A surprising number of our common vegetables are descended from the wild cabbage, which still grows around the coasts of Europe. The ancient Greeks, Romans, Saxons, and Celts cultivated some varieties of it, and all of those we eat today are varieties of the one species.

The varieties we eat include cabbages, which may be round and green or red, or of the savoy type, with wrinkled leaves. Round cabbages are often cut early and used before their hearts have formed. There are also flowering cabbages, developed in Japan and grown for ornament, but of the same variety as curled, or curly, kale. Ordinary kale is a different variety: it has a stronger flavor than curly kale and

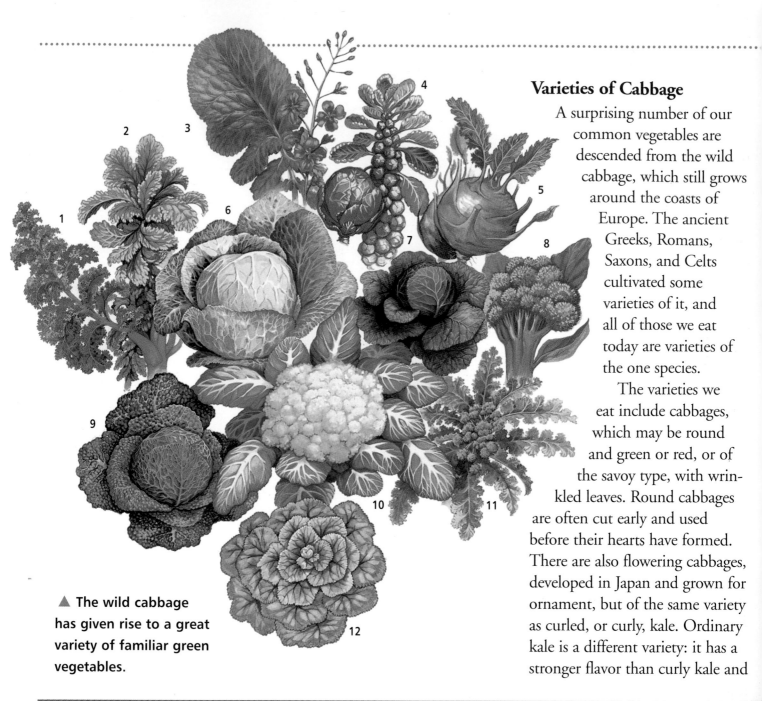

▲ The wild cabbage has given rise to a great variety of familiar green vegetables.

RELATIVES OF THE CABBAGE

Common name	Scientific name	Common name	Scientific name	Common name	Scientific name
1 Curled kale	*Brassica oleracea* var. *acephala*	6 Round cabbage	*B. oleracea* vars. *capitata, bullata, sabauda*	10 Cauliflower	*B. oleracea* var. *botrytis*
2 Kale	*B. oleracea* var. *medullosa*	7 Red cabbage	*B. oleracea* vars. *capitata, bullata, sabauda*	11 Purple sprouting broccoli	*B. oleracea* var. *botrytis*
3 Wild cabbage	*B. oleracea*			12 Flowering cabbage	*B. oleracea* var. *acephala*
4 Brussels sprouts	*B. oleracea* var. *gemmifera*	8 Green broccoli	*B. oleracea* var. *italica*		
5 Kohlrabi	*B. oleracea* var. *gongylodes*	9 Savoy cabbage	*B. oleracea* vars. *capitata, bullata, sabauda*	Bok choy	*B. chinensis*
				Chinese cabbage	*B. pekinensis*

is often grown to be eaten by farm livestock. Brussels sprouts, yet another variety, are grown for their buds, which resemble tiny cabbages and form in the axils—the angles between the stem and leaves. They were first grown near Brussels, Belgium, possibly as early as about 1200 A.D.

We eat the leaves of cabbages and sprouts, but the flower buds of cauliflower and broccoli. They have been bred to produce a densely packed head of tiny flower buds. Cauliflower and purple sprouting broccoli form one variety, green sprouting broccoli, or calabrese, forms another. In the case of kohlrabi we eat the swollen base of the stem, which resembles a turnip, so it is sometimes called the turnip-rooted cabbage.

Eggplant, Avocado, Breadfruit, and Jack fruit

Some of our vegetables originated in the tropics. The most familiar is probably the eggplant, originally from tropical Asia but now grown outside the tropics, sometimes in greenhouses. It is called an eggplant because of the shape of its fruit, which is the part we eat. Eggplants are always cooked before eating.

Avocados originated in Central America, but are now grown as far north as Florida and California, and around the Mediterranean.

▲ Young Brussels sprouts plants growing commercially in a large field. Many of the sprouts will be frozen to preserve them.

We eat the raw fruit. Avocados are highly nutritious, containing more protein than any other fruit. Twenty-five percent of their weight is fat, and they are rich in vitamins A and B.

Breadfruit grows on the islands of the Pacific, and jack fruit grows on the Asian mainland. Neither is eaten very much outside the regions where it grows, although breadfruit has been planted in many parts of the tropics. In 1787 HMS *Bounty* was carrying breadfruit plants from Tahiti to be grown in the West Indies when the famous mutiny against Captain Bligh took place. Breadfruit is eaten cooked. Jack fruits, which can weigh up to 70 pounds (32 kg), can be eaten either cooked or raw.

Melons, Squashes, Marrows, and Cucumbers

Melons, squashes, and cucumbers are fruits. They all belong to the same plant family. Some are eaten as vegetables, others as dessert.

See Also | *MUSTARD FAMILY* **10** 20 ◉

▶ Squashes and cucumbers are grown in a wide range of shapes and sizes.

◀ Many tropical vegetables have become popular in temperate regions. Others, such as breadfruit and jack fruit, are less well known outside the tropics.

Although they are now rare, wild cucumbers grow in the Himalayas and southwestern China. It is likely they were first cultivated in India, and the ancient Greeks and Romans ate them. Most gherkins are small, unripe cucumbers, but the true gherkin is a different species that grows wild in the West Indies, as a weed. It is cultivated in tropical and subtropical America, and its small fruits are picked unripe and preserved by pickling.

Closely related to cucumbers, melons are eaten at the start of a meal or as dessert. They came originally from West Africa and are now grown in most of the warmer parts of the world. Honeydew melons have pale green flesh and a smooth skin. The skin of netted or musk melons is covered by a network of pale, raised ridges. Cantaloupe melons have an uneven skin and orange flesh. Watermelons belong to the same family, but are of a different genus. They originated in tropical Africa and are now

SUBTROPICAL AND TROPICAL VEGETABLES

Common name	Scientific name	Common name	Scientific name
1 Eggplant	*Solanum melongena*	5 Bamboo shoots	*Bambusa* and *Phyllostachis* species, especially *B. vulgaris* and *P. pubescens*
2 Okra	*Abelmoschus esculentus*		
3 Breadfruit	*Artocarpus altilis*	6 Endive	*Cichorium endiva*
4 Avocado	*Persea americana*	7 Jack fruit	*Artocarpus heterophyllus*

MARROWS, GOURDS, AND THEIR RELATIVES

Common name	Scientific name	Common name	Scientific name	Common name	Scientific name
1 Netted melon	Cucumis melo var. reticulatus	7 Honeydew melon	Cucumis melo var. saccharinus	Cantaloupe	Cucumis melo var. cantalupensis
2 Cucumber	Cucumis sativus	8 Pattypan squash	Cucurbita pepo	Gherkin	Cucumis anguria
3 Zucchini	Cucurbita pepo	9 Watermelon	Citrullus lanatus	Malabar gourd	Cucurbita ficifolia
4 Summer squash	Cucurbita pepo	10 Vegetable marrow	Cucurbita pepo	Missouri gourd	Cucurbita foetidissima
5 Pumpkin	Cucurbita moschata			Vegetable spaghetti	Cucurbita pepo
6 Winter squash	Cucurbita mixta	Bottle gourd	Lagenaria siceraria	West Indian gherkin	Cucumis anguria
		Butternut squash	Cucurbita moschata		
		Calabash	Lagenaria siceraria		

See Also | CUCUMBER FAMILY **10** 18 👁

naturalized in tropical America.

Squashes are cooked and eaten as vegetables. They are all descended from a plant that grew in Central and South America and probably resembled the pumpkin. It was domesticated independently in both Central and South America and, with beans and corn, formed the basis of the diet of Americans prior to the arrival of Europeans. While many varieties of squashes are grown in America, fewer are grown in Europe. A type of pumpkin, known as a marrow, is cultivated, and the very small version of it, called a courgette (French) or zucchini (Italian), is highly popular.

Beans, Lentils, and Peas

Peas and beans belong to a very large plant family, the Fabaceae, all of which produce seeds in pods. The groundnut (peanut) belongs to this family, but differs

▼ Peas being poured into a trailer from a combine harvester on a farm in Oregon.

▲ Peas and beans are the seeds of their plants. They are rich in protein.

from the others in that its flowers grow at ground level or even below it. Once the flower has been pollinated, the flower stalk lengthens, pushing the young seed pods into the ground, where they mature. So groundnuts have to be dug up—hence their name.

Groundnuts grow only in warm climates, and they are the most important crop in many countries. Other members of the

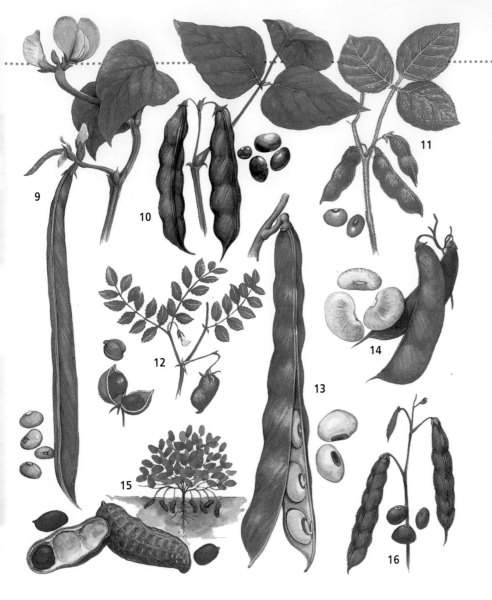

▲ **Peas, beans, and groundnuts all belong to the same plant family, the Fabaceae.**

family are cultivated throughout the temperate regions as well.

Runner beans, French beans, kidney beans, haricot beans, butter beans, and several other varieties are all descended from plants that grow naturally in the warmer parts of America. Except for runner and French beans, the pod is inedible, and it is the seeds that are eaten. The broad bean is different. It was first cultivated in southwestern Asia and came to be grown throughout Europe.

A third group of small beans are called grams, from a Portuguese word derived from the Latin *granum,* meaning grain. They originated in tropical Asia and India, where they are still grown. They are boiled to make a kind of porridge. The Latin for porridge is *puls,* so beans cooked this way are known as pulses. The chickpea, or Bengal gram, is the most widely grown. Adzuki and mung beans can also be sprouted and are eaten as bean sprouts.

Lentils, also eaten as pulses, originated in southwestern Asia. They are still widely grown around the Mediterranean. The garden pea is a native of the Near East. It is now grown on a large scale in North America and Europe. Most peas are harvested by machines, packed, and frozen quickly to preserve them. The sugar pea variety (known as mangetout in Europe) has pods that can be eaten whole.

Root Crops

WE EAT MANY PARTS OF THE VEGETABLE PLANTS WE CULTIVATE: the leaves, flowers, seeds, fruit, or roots. Among root crops the potato is an important staple food in the diets of many people. As well as being tasty and nutritious, root vegetables can be stored and eaten through the winter, when the season for other vegetables has ended.

Potatoes grow naturally on the western slopes of the Andes, in Peru and Bolivia. This region is within the tropics, but potatoes grow at 8,000 feet (2,440 m) above sea level, where the climate is temperate. People there were eating wild potatoes about 8,000 years ago, and by 2,000 years ago potatoes were being farmed.

Potatoes were brought to Spain in about 1570. They were probably among the supplies taken to feed the crew of a ship sailing from the port of Cartagena, Colombia. By the end of the 16th century they were being grown throughout Europe and had become an important food crop in Ireland by the middle of the 17th century. The first potatoes to be planted in North America (in New Hampshire in 1719) came from Irish seed stock. More were introduced in New York State in 1851, this time from Colombia.

Tubers

There are many varieties of potatoes, but they all belong to a single species. The potatoes we cook and eat are tubers. Although they grow below ground, they are not the roots of the plant, but swellings at the tips of underground stems, called rhizomes. Each year the parts of the plant above ground die and disappear. The tubers are stores of food that nourish the plant when it grows again the following season.

Other South American tubers are rarely seen outside their native regions. The oca, for example, is cultivated in Bolivia, Peru, and Ecuador. Its tubers are very acid when fresh and are usually dried in the Sun for a few days, which improves their flavor. Unlike the potato (the leaves of which are poisonous), the green parts of the oca can be eaten either cooked or raw in salads. The ulluco of western South America produces

▶ **Arrowroot, sweet potato, and taro are among the tropical root vegetables.**

▼ **Potatoes, carrots, and parsnips are among the roots that grow in temperate climates.**

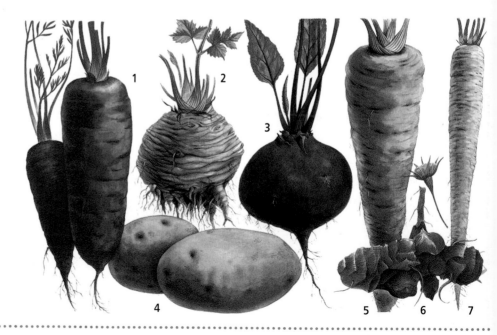

ROOT VEGETABLES

Common name	Scientific name	Common name	Scientific name	Common name	Scientific name
1 Carrot	*Daucus carota sativus*	6 Jerusalem artichoke	*Helianthus tuberosus*	12 Cassava	*Manihot utilissima*
2 Celeriac	*Apium graveolens var. rapaceum*	7 Salsify	*Tragopogon porrifolius*	13 Oca	*Oxalis tuberosa*
3 Beet	*Beta vulgaris*	8 Arrowroot	*Maranta arundinacea*	14 Yam bean	*Pachyrrhizus erosus*
4 Potato	*Solanum tuberosum*	9 Sweet potato	*Ipomoea batatas*	15 Taro	*Colocasia esculenta*
5 Parsnip	*Pastinaca sativa*	10 Yam	*Dioscorea* species	16 Anu	*Tropaeolum tuberosum*
		11 Ulluco	*Ullucus tuberosus*	17 Tanier	*Xanthosomas sagittifolium*

See Also | VEGETATIVE REPRODUCTION **2** 46 │ CARROT FAMILY **10** 38 │ POTATO FAMILY **10** 40 👁

small, starchy tubers, not unlike potatoes. The tubers of Jerusalem artichokes can also be peeled and cooked like potatoes

Sweet potatoes, yams, and yam beans also produce edible tubers. Sweet potatoes belong to the convolvulus family (Convolvulaceae) and are not closely related to ordinary potatoes. Originally from South America, they now grow as far north as New Jersey. Yams belong to the Dioscoreaceae family, and most of the edible species originate from Africa or Asia. Yam beans are from tropical America and belong to the bean family (Fabaceae). As their name suggests, they produce edible pods of seeds as well as tubers.

Cassava, Arrowroot, and Taro

Cassava, also called manioc, mandioca, or tapioca, is an important tropical food. A native of tropical America, where it has been grown for at least 4,000 years, it is now cultivated in parts of Africa and Asia as well.

The cassava plant is a small tree, up to 9 feet (2.7 m) tall, belonging to the spurge family (Euphorbiaceae). The edible parts are the swollen, tapering roots. They are about 8 inches (20 cm) across, up to 3 feet (90 cm) long, and rich in starch. They have little protein though, so a diet based on cassava is likely to be unbalanced. The many varieties can be divided into two broad types, bitter or sweet. The bitterness is due to the quantities of cyanide the roots contain. The cyanide makes the entire plant toxic to insect pests, including locusts, which is an advantage, but it must be removed from the roots before the cassava can be eaten. To do this the roots are soaked in water, squeezed partly dry, then dried in the Sun. Dried cassava can be grated to make a kind of flour (called farinha in Brazil and garri in West Africa) that is cooked in small cakes.

Arrowroot is more nutritious because its swollen rhizomes contain protein and minerals as well as starch. The rhizomes are peeled, washed, grated into water, washed several times, and finally dried. This produces a food that is very easily digested. It is often given to infants and invalids. Arrowroot is native to tropical America, but it is grown commercially mainly in St. Vincent, in the West Indies.

The crop that is called taro in the islands of the Pacific, eddo or dasheen in the West Indies, and cocoyam in West Africa is a native of tropical Asia that is grown on a small scale in many parts of the tropics. The edible part is the swollen base of the stem, known as a corm, that forms below ground. It is rich in starch and easily digested.

Carrots and Other Taproots

Carrots are true roots. Wild carrots grow in many parts of the world. They have small, pale, tough taproots. Carrots with yellow roots were first domesticated in Afghanistan. Western varieties with red or orange roots were bred from early varieties, and the ancient Greeks and Romans ate them. Their color is due to the presence of red anthocyanins and orange carotene. Carotene is converted to vitamin A by the process of digestion.

Parsnips are similar in shape to carrots and belong to the same family (Apiaceae), but tend to be much bigger. Like carrots, they are taproots, and the cultivated varieties are descended from wild plants that still grow in many parts of Europe. The Romans grew parsnips, and the plants were introduced to North America early in the 17th century.

Celery is another member of the carrot and parsnip family. One variety of celery is cultivated for its root rather than its leaf stalks. It is called celeriac and is eaten boiled or raw and grated in salads. It tastes like celery, but slightly anisey.

▶ A field of potatoes. The soil is heaped into long ridges around the plants to stimulate growth of the tubers and prevent them turning green.

Oil Crops

VEGETABLE OILS ARE FAMILIAR FROM THEIR EVERYDAY USES. They are used to make food dressings, margarine and other spreads, as well as high-quality soaps. In ancient times plant oils, especially olive oil, were burned in lamps. They provided the only source of lighting on dark evenings.

Olives have been cultivated to the north of the Dead Sea for more than 5,500 years. The oil, obtained by pressing the ripe fruits, is used for cooking, as a flavoring, and as a preservative. Olive oil is also used in some soaps and cosmetics, and in the past it was burned in lamps.

The olive has always been regarded as a special plant. Only olive oil was deemed suitable for use in the sanctuary lamps that burned night and day. It was used to anoint rulers and priests. The presentation of an olive branch was—and is still—an indication of a desire to make peace.

Groundnuts, Sesame, Walnuts, and Oil Palm

Olive oil is produced in many parts of the world, but olive trees will grow only in a subtropical or warm-temperate climate like that of the Mediterranean or southern California. Many oil-producing plants require a warm climate.

Groundnuts, or peanuts, are grown for their oil. Originally from South America, they are cultivated as far north as Virginia and in Africa and Asia. Unlike olives, which are the fruit of a long-lived tree, the groundnut plant is an annual, so a new crop is grown every year. Soya, a plant of Asian origin, is another annual crop grown for its oil. As well as being edible, soya oil has many industrial uses in soaps, paints, and plastics.

Sesame crops yield less oil than other plants, but the oil has a distinctive flavor that many people like. The plant, a native of Africa, is now grown over a wide area, especially in Asia. Its oil is extracted from the seeds, which are also used in confectionery and to decorate bread and cakes.

Walnut oil, which is obtained by pressing the nuts, also has an individual flavor. Walnut trees grow in temperate regions. The oil palm is cultivated in

◀ **Fields filled with the bright yellow flowers of oilseed rape make splashes of vivid color in the landscape.**

Many of the plants that are cultivated for their oil need a warm, sunny climate.

plantations in tropical Africa and Asia. The oil, obtained from the layer of tissue beneath the skin of the fruit, is commercial palm oil. At the center of the fruit the seed contains a more valuable oil, called palm-kernel oil.

of cabbages, has also been cultivated for centuries. When its yellow flowers disappear, the dry fruits form. Up to 4 inches (10 cm) long, they hold the seeds from which the oil is pressed.

Flax is also grown for its oil, known as linseed oil. The variety cultivated as an oil crop has small blue flowers.

Colorful Crops

Three crops—sunflower, rape, and linseed—dominate vegetable oil production in the temperate climates of North America and Europe, and bring bright colors to the countryside.

Each sunflower is made up of many small florets. They attract bees looking for pollen, so sunflowers yield honey as well as edible seeds and oil. Sunflowers probably originated in North America or Mexico and were being grown in Europe in the 16th century.

Rape, or canola, a close relative

OIL CROPS

Common name	Scientific name	Common name	Scientific name
1 Castor oil	Ricinus communis	Chaulmoogra	Hydnocarpus pentandra
2 Coconut	Cocos nucifera		
3 Sesame	Sesamum indicum	Cocoa	Theobroma cacao
4 Olive	Olea europaea	Cohune	Orbignya cohune
5 Oil palm	Elaeis guineensis	Cotton	Gossypium species
6 Sunflower	Helianthus annuus	Croton	Croton tiglium
		Hemp seed	Cannabis sativa
Almond	Prunus dulcis	Kapok seed	Ceiba pentandra
Andiroba	Carapa guianensis	Flax (linseed)	Linum usitatissimum
Babassú	Orbignya barbosiana	Macassar	Schleichera oleosa
Ben	Moringa oleifera	Pistachio	Pistacia vera
Brazil nut	Bertholletia excelsa	Rape	Brassica napus
Candlenut	Aleurites moluccana	Safflower	Carthamus tinctorius
Cashew nut	Anacardium occidentale	Soya	Glycine max
		Tung	Aleurites montana

See Also | *VEGETABLES 5* 16 | *PALM FAMILY 9* 30 | *SUNFLOWER FAMILY 10* 46 👁

Sugar and Starch Crops

MANY DIFFERENT TYPES OF PLANTS are grown for the sugar they produce. Plants store sugar in the form of starch. A starch molecule consists of many sugar molecules joined together. When we digest starch, the molecules are separated, so the starch is converted to sugar.

Sugar cane is the source of more than half of all the sugar eaten in the world. It is a grass that originated in tropical Asia and was introduced in America.

Stems of cane take about a year to grow to their full size. Then the leaves and upper parts of the plant are removed, sometimes by setting fire to the entire crop, after which the stems, or canes, are cut. They are rich in sugar, which is extracted by a complex process.

▼ Sugar and starch are obtained from many kinds of plants, including maple trees, palm trees, cycads, root crops, and grasses.

SUGAR AND STARCH

Common name	Scientific name
1 Sugar cane	Saccharum officinarum
2 Sugar maple	Acer saccharum
3 Wild date palm	Phoenix sylvestris
4 Sugar palm	Arenga pinnata
5 Sugar beet	Beta vulgaris
6 Toddy palm	Caryota urens
Asiatic yam	Dioscorea alata
Black maple	Acer nigrum
Cabbage palm	Oreodoxa oleracea
Cush-cush yam	Dioscorea trifida
Date palm	Phoenix dactylifera
East Indian arrowroot	Curcuma angustifolia
Honey palm	Jubaea chilensis
Japanese sago palm	Cycas revoluta
Corn (maize)	Zea mays
Manna ash	Fraxinus ornus
Nypa palm	Nypa fruticans
Palmyra palm	Borassus flabellifer
Queen sago	Cycas circinalis
Queensland arrowroot	Canna edulis
Sago palm	Metroxylon rumphii or M. sagu
Sweet sorghum	Sorghum bicolor
White yam	Dioscorea rotundata
Yellow yam	Dioscorea cayenensis

New canes grow from where the first crop was cut, but after a few years yields start to decline. New stems are then planted, and the cycle is repeated.

Sugar Beet

In temperate climates sugar beet replaces sugar cane as the most important sugar crop. Sugar is obtained from taproots that average 14 inches (36 cm) in length and weigh about 2 pounds (900 g). The roots are shredded and washed in hot running water, from which the sugar is extracted.

Sugar from Trees

Sugar and black maple trees are grown in North America for their sap, known as maple syrup, a rich source of sugar. Most trees grown for sugar in the tropics are palms, such as the palmyra or borassus palm, the wild date palm, and the nypa and sugar palms that grow wild in southern Asia.

Sago, a type of starch, is obtained from several different plants. The most important, the sago palm, grows wild in south-eastern Asia. The cabbage palm of tropical America also yields sago.

Other crops grown for their starch include corn (maize), yams, potatoes, cassava, and arrowroot.

▶ Sometimes, as here, sugar cane is burned to remove the leaves before harvesting.

See Also | *CEREALS* **5** *12* | *GRASS FAMILY* **9** *12* | *PALM FAMILY* **9** *30* 👁

Fibers

NOT ALL THE CROPS THAT FARMERS PRODUCE are grown for food. Some are grown for their fibers, which are used to make such everyday things as cloth, rope and string, baskets, fishing nets, thatching for roofs, mats, chair seats, and paper. Plant fibers are also used for packing breakable items during transportation.

Cotton was cultivated 6,000 years ago by people living at Mohenjo-Daro in northern India. When Hernando Cortés landed in Mexico in 1519, he found people wearing cotton garments. Cotton has also been found in the ruins of prehistoric pueblo buildings in Arizona.

Several species of cotton plants are cultivated, all belonging to the same genus. Each cotton fiber is a single cell that is 1,000 to 3,000 times longer than it is wide. It develops from the outer layer of the seed of the plant, enclosing the seed in a ball of fibers called a boll. The fibers dry when they are exposed to the air, and at this stage they are called lint. The process of separating the seed from the lint is called ginning. At one time the bolls were picked and ginned by hand, but now the operations are mechanized. After ginning, the lint is spun into yarn from which cloth is woven.

Linen

People living in countries now known as Israel, Jordan, and Syria

▲ Picking cotton by machine in California. The work was formerly done by hand.

were growing flax 8,000 years ago. From there cultivation spread to ancient Egypt and then to other parts of Africa, Europe, and Asia.

The flax plant grown for fiber has white flowers. It grows to a height of about 3 feet (90 cm), and it is from the main stem that the fiber is obtained. It is harvested by pulling the plant from the ground, then submerging it in

water. This process, called retting, stiffens and loosens the outer bark of the stem, allowing it to be crushed and then removed. This leaves the long, straight, flax fibers that are spun into yarn from which linen cloth is woven.

Cotton and linen are fine fabrics, suitable for making a wide variety of garments as well as household items that are traditionally known as linen. They are not necessarily delicate fabrics, however. Until synthetic fibers replaced them, sails for ships were made from linen or cotton.

Jute

Coarser materials, used to make sacks and matting, are derived from jute plants, of which there are several species. There are now substitutes, but genuine hessian, burlap, and sacking are made from jute, as is tarpaulin.

Jute originated in India, and today it is grown mainly on small farms there and in Bangladesh. Each plant produces a single stem, about 1 inch (2.5 cm) thick and 6–15 feet (1.8–4.6 m) tall. After

▲ Many crops are grown for their fibers, but by far the most important are cotton (2) and flax (6).

harvesting, the fiber is released in much the same way as flax fibers.

Hemp

Jute can be made into rope, but hemp, from the stem of the plant, is the best natural fiber for this purpose. In North America Indian hemp and hemp dogbane were once used by Native Americans to make cords and cloth. Hemp fibers, like those of esparto grass and some bamboos, can be made into paper.

FIBER CROPS

Common name	Scientific name	Common name	Scientific name
1 Hemp	*Cannabis sativa*	Albardine	*Lygeum spartum*
2 Cotton	*Gossypium* species	Bamboo	*Bambusa* species
3 Manila hemp	*Musa textilis*	Bowstring hemp	*Sanseviera cylindrica*
4 Jute	*Corchorus* species	Hemp dogbane	*Apocynum venetum*
5 Sisal	*Agave sisalana*	Indian hemp	*Apocynum cannabinum*
6 Flax	*Linum usitatissimum*		
7 Raffia	*Raphia hookeri*	Kenaf	*Hibiscus cannabinus*
8 Kapok	*Ceiba pentandra*	Malacca cane	*Calamus* species
9 Dwarf fan palm	*Chamaerops humilis*	Swamp milkweed	*Asclepias incarnata*
10 Esparto grass	*Stipa tenacissima*	New Zealand flax	*Phormium tenax*
11 Ramie	*Boehmeria nivea*	Panama hat palm	*Carludovica palmata*
12 Pineapple	*Ananas comosus*	Rattan cane	*Daemonorops* species, *Calamus* species, and *Korthalsia* species
13 Coconut, coir	*Cocos nucifera*		
		Stinging nettle	*Urtica dioica*
		Sunn hemp	*Crotalaria juncea*

See Also | *CELL TYPES AND TISSUES* **1** *18* | *STEMS* **1** *28* | *PALM FAMILY* **9** *30* 👁

Flavorings from Plants

PEPPER, MUSTARD, CHILI, VANILLA, PEPPERMINT, THYME, AND OREGANO are a few familiar examples of the many flavorings we obtain from plants. In the quantities used they have no nutritional value, but they have been extremely important throughout history. They can make dull, tasteless, or even foul-tasting food edible, and ordinary dishes extraordinary.

Generally the leaves of herbs are used for flavoring and, in a few cases, the stems. Herbs have been grown in separate gardens for many centuries. Because many of them have also been used as medicinal remedies, they were grown for this purpose in physic gardens—"physic" is an old word for medicine.

An herb garden might contain parsley, chervil, myrrh or sweet cicely, and samphire, all of which are umbellifers (family Apiaceae). It might also have a range of mints, oregano, sage, marjoram, rosemary, basil, savory, lemon balm, and different varieties of thyme, which belong to the mint family (Lamiaceae), as well as tarragon, tansy, and chamomile, which are members of the sunflower family (Asteraceae).

Valuable Spices

Spices, such as cloves, nutmeg, chili, cinnamon, and turmeric, usually grow only in the tropics. The parts of the plant to be used are usually dried, but it varies: vanilla flavoring, for example, is extracted from the long, narrow, fruit pod of a climbing orchid. It grows naturally in Central America and was used by the Aztecs to flavor cocoa. Allspice (also known as pimenta and Jamaica pepper) is obtained from the unripe berries of a small, tropical American tree. Chili powder is made from the dried fruits of a variety of capsicum. They are the only spices that are native to America, although nowadays they are grown in other parts of the world as well.

Most other spices originated in southern Asia, many of them on islands in or near what is now Indonesia, and especially the Moluccas. They were once known as the Spice Islands because of two types of tree that at one time grew there and nowhere else. One tree yielded cloves, and the other yielded nutmeg and mace. They were such valuable commodities that Portugal had control of trade in the islands for 100 years, and for 200 years after that The Netherlands controlled them.

Mace and nutmeg come from the same plant. The seed is enclosed in a fleshy (but inedible) fruit that splits open when it is ripe to reveal the nutmeg (the seed), wrapped in a red, fleshy, netlike structure called an aril. Carefully removed, it is flattened, then dried, which turns it an orange-brown color. It is known as mace and is used to flavor savory dishes such as sauces and ketchup. Nutmeg is usually used with sweet dishes. Cloves are dried flower buds and are added to both meat and sweet dishes.

Saffron is an unusual spice and one of the most expensive of all traded commodities. It consists of the styles of a particular crocus flower. Styles, which in this flower have three branches, are the stalklike structures linking the stigma and ovary of the flower. Saffron imparts a distinctive flavor to foods such as rice, bouillabaisse (a fish stew), cakes, and bread, and also colors them yellow. It was formerly used as a dye for fabrics

HERBS

	Common name	Scientific name
1	Garden thyme	*Thymus vulgaris*
2	Sweet marjoram	*Origanum majorana*
3	Parsley	*Petroselinum crispum*
4	Coriander	*Coriandrum sativum*
5	Sage	*Salvia officinalis*
6	Rosemary	*Rosmarinus officinalis*
7	Chervil	*Anthriscus cerefolium*
8	Tarragon	*Artemisia dracunculus*
9	Peppermint	*Mentha x piperita*
10	Summer savory	*Satureja hortensis*
11	Fennel	*Foeniculum vulgare*
12	Sweet basil	*Ocimum basilicum*
13	Dill	*Anethum graveolens*
14	Tansy	*Tanacetum vulgare*
15	Spearmint	*Mentha spicata*
16	Lemon balm	*Melissa officinalis*
17	Lovage	*Levisticum officinale*
18	Costmary	*Balsamita major*
	Alexanders	*Smyrnium olusatrum*
	Angelica	*Angelica archangelica*
	Chamomile	*Chamaemelum nobile*
	Chives	*Allium schoenoprasum*
	Hyssop	*Hyssopus officinalis*
	Lemon grass	*Cymbopogon citratus*
	Lemon verbena	*Aloysia triphylla*
	Myrrh	*Myrrhis odorata*
	Oregano	*Origanum vulgare*
	Rocket	*Eruca sativa*
	Samphire	*Crithmum maritimum*
	Sweet woodruff	*Galium odoratum*

◄ **Most herbs grow in temperate climates. Their leaves, stems, or flowers are used fresh or dried.**

See Also | ORCHID FAMILY **9** *16* | MINT FAMILY **10** *42* | SUNFLOWER FAMILY **10** *46*

and cosmetics. Saffron is expensive because it must be picked by hand, and it takes 454,000 flowers to produce one pound of dried saffron; or one million flowers to produce one kilogram.

Flavoring for Curries

India and Sri Lanka are famous for their spicy dishes. Curries acquire their color and some of their flavor from turmeric, an Indian plant. It is related to ginger, which is also used in curries, and in both cases it is the tubers—underground storage organs—that are used.

Cardamom, another spice used in flavoring curries, is grown mainly in India and Sri Lanka. The spice is obtained from the seeds. To preserve the seeds' delicate flavor, the plant's fruits are harvested before they ripen, then gently dried. The seeds are then removed from the fruits.

Cinnamon is used to flavor confectionery as well as curries. It is the bark of a tree that grows to a height of about 60 feet (18 m) in the wild, but in cultivation it is grown from seed to produce shoots that are cut when they are about two years old. The bark is removed from the shoots in two long strips, the outer layer is scraped away, and the strips slowly dried. They curl as they dry and can be folded one inside another for ease of packing.

Nowadays, chilies are used to give curries their piquancy, or hot flavor, but chilies were introduced to southern Asia only in the 16th century. Until then pepper—obtained from an Indian climbing plant grown on a trellis—was used. Of all the spices, pepper has always been the most important in terms of world trade.

Peppers—peppercorns—are the dried fruits of the plant. They form in long spikes that hang from the stem. Some are picked before they ripen and dried slowly in the Sun, their surfaces wrinkling as they do so. They are known as black peppers. Others are picked when the fruits are ripe. The fruits are soaked, after which their outer coatings are rubbed off, leaving behind the seeds. They are white peppers.

Although it is grown in Asia, cumin originally came from lands around the Mediterranean. The fruits are used for flavoring and are similar to caraway. Both plants have flowers that are grouped into a parasol shape, called an umbel, and they belong to the group of plants known as umbellifers (formerly known as the family Umbelliferae, now as Apiaceae). This large family includes a number with fruits and seeds that are used as spices. Coriander, dill, and fennel are umbellifers, and all are natives of Europe and temperate parts of Asia.

SPICES	
Common name	Scientific name
1 Caraway	Carum carvi
2 Anise	Pimpinella anisum
3 Cumin	Cuminum cyminum
4 Allspice	Pimenta dioica
5 Bay	Laurus nobilis
6 Capers	Capparis spinosa
7 Saffron	Crocus sativus
8 Cloves	Syzygium aromaticum
9 Vanilla	Vanilla planifolia
10 Turmeric	Curcuma domestica
11 Sorrel	Rumex acetosa
12 Tarragon	Artemisia dracunculus
13 Nutmeg	Myristica fragrans
14 Mace	Myristica fragrans
15 Ginger	Zingiber officinale
16 Cardamom	Elettaria cardamomum
17 Pepper	Piper nigrum
18 Cinnamon	Cinnamomum zeylanicum
19 Fenugreek	Trigonella foenum-graecum
20 Chili	Capsicum frutescens
21 Juniper	Juniperus communis
22 Licorice	Glycyrrhiza glabra
Angostura	Cusparia febrifuga
Horseradish	Armoracia rusticana
Mustard	Brassica juncea or Sinapis alba
Poppy	Papaver somniferum, Glaucium flavum, or Argemone glauca
Sarsaparilla	Smilax species
Sassafras	Sassafras albidum
Sesame	Sesamum indicum
Tamarind	Tamarindus indica

▶ **Most spices grow in the tropics. Their seeds, bark, flowers, or fruits are used dried.**

1

2

3

4

5

6

7

8

9

10

11

12

13

14

15

16

17

18

19

20

21

22

Beverages

A BEVERAGE IS A DRINK THAT USES INGREDIENTS OR FLAVORINGS derived from part of a plant. Many fruits can be crushed to yield thirst-quenching juices, but to produce a beverage, the raw ingredients must be altered in some way. Drinks such as coffee, tea, cocoa, beer, and wine are among the most widely consumed beverages.

Three of the most common beverages—coffee, tea, and cocoa—have been around for a long time. Coffee is made from the roasted seeds, or beans, of an evergreen shrub that grows naturally in parts of East Africa. No one knows how it came to be domesticated, but it occurs in legends dating from 850 A.D. In fact, coffee was probably being grown in southern Arabia by about 1500 A.D.

The coffee bush produces berries that turn red as they ripen. Each berry contains one or more (usually two) beans. Ripe berries may be opened by a machine and the beans left in water for about 24 hours to ferment slightly before being dried in the Sun for two to three weeks. This produces mild coffee, which is of the highest quality. Alternatively, the berries are dried first, and then machines separate the beans from the pulp. This produces hard coffee, which is of poorer quality.

Tea and Cocoa

Tea was first cultivated in China, probably more than 2,500 years ago. Its Chinese name is pronounced "chah" in the Cantonese dialect, and this word traveled to Japan, the Middle East, and Russia. In the Amoy dialect the same word is pronounced "tay." It is this word, brought to western Europe by Dutch merchants, that was used until the 18th century.

The beverage is made from the dried, crushed leaves of a small shrub. Only the youngest, most tender leaves are used. They are handpicked from the tips of the branches. They are then partly dried and rolled to break open the leaf cells, after which drying is completed. The leaves are fermented before the final drying to produce black tea, steamed and only lightly rolled to produce green tea, and partly fermented to produce oolong tea. The tea is then cut, sifted, and graded before being packed.

Cocoa is produced from the seeds of a tropical American plant. The seeds are almost always processed in the countries that import them.

◀ Tea is made from the young leaves at the tips of the branches of tea bushes. This tea plantation is in South Africa.

▲ Wine grapes are grown on rows of small vines. This vineyard is in South Africa.

Alcoholic Beverages

Other beverages are made by fermenting a liquid that contains sugar. Fermentation, by a yeast, converts the sugar into alcohol. Grape juice is fermented to make wine. All wine grapes belong to the same species, but there are hundreds of varieties.

Part-germination of barley grains converts some of the starch to sugar. Roasting halts the process to produce malt, containing the sugar maltose. It is dissolved in water and fermented to make beer (flavored with hops), and whiskey. Rye and corn can be processed in the same way.

BEVERAGES		
Drink	**Plant source**	**Scientific name**
Akvavit	potato and caraway	*Solanum tuberosum* and *Carum carvi*
Beer	barley and hops	*Hordeum vulgare* and *Humulus lupulus*
Chicory	chicory plant	*Cichorium intybus*
Cider	apple	*Malus pumila*
Cocoa	cocoa tree	*Theobroma cacao*
Coffee	coffee bush	*Coffea arabica, C. canephora,* or *C. liberica*
Dandelion coffee	dandelion	*Taraxacum officinale*
Ginger beer	ginger	*Zingiber officinale*
Kvass	barley, rye, or mint	*Hordeum vulgare, Secale cereale,* or *Mentha* species
Maté	maté tree	*Ilex paraguariensis*
Mescal	agave	*Agave* species
Pulque	agave	*Agave* species
Rum	sugar cane	*Saccharum officinarum*
Saké	rice	*Oryza sativa*
Tea	tea bush	*Camellia sinensis*
Whiskey	barley, rye, or corn	*Hordeum vulgare, Secale cereale,* or *Zea mays*
Wine	grape vine	*Vitis vinifera*

See Also | GRASS FAMILY **9** 12 👁

Medicinal Plants

MOST PLANTS MANUFACTURE SUBSTANCES that are harmful to predators. The domesticated plants that we eat are no longer poisonous as a result of many generations of selection, or they are descended from ancestors that were not poisonous. Many wild plants remain poisonous, however. Certain plant toxins, when used in very small doses, can help alleviate illnesses. They are medicines.

For thousands of years people have known that certain plants, when eaten or used as a salve, will relieve symptoms of illness. Many animals also seek out particular plants when ill.

Feverfew is an herb that grows wild in most of Europe. In medieval times it was grown in "physic" (medicine) gardens. People discovered that a drink made with dried feverfew flowers would reduce a fever, chewing the bark of certain willow trees would cure a headache, and that juice extracted from the unripe fruit of certain poppies would relieve fevers and severe pain.

Identifying Herbal Medicines

Throughout the world people have always used local plants to cure their ailments. As trade developed between continents, the best of the remedies came to be used far from the lands in which they grew naturally. Doctors relied on herbal remedies, accumulating knowledge about effective treatments over centuries.

During the first half of the 19th century scientists experimented with treatments to discover how they produced their effects. Chemists then began to isolate the substances responsible. They found that willow bark contains salicilin, which has an effect like

MEDICINAL PLANTS

Common name	Scientific name	Active ingredient	Use
American black birch	Betula lenta	Methyl salicylate	Pain relief
Belladonna	Atropa belladonna	Atropine	Sedative; pupil dilation
Camphor	Cinnamomum camphora	Camphor	Antiseptic
Cascara	Rhamnus purshiana	Cascara sagrada	Purgative
Coca	Erythroxylum coca	Cocaine	Local anesthetic
Cocoa	Theobroma cacao	Theobromine	Diuretic
Ephedra	Ephedra sinica, or E. distachya	Ephedrine	Relief of bronchial spasm
Feverfew	Tanacetum parthenium		Reducing temperature
Henbane	Hyoscyamus niger	Hyoscyamine	Sedative
Indian snakeroot	Rauvolffia serpentina	Reserpine	High blood pressure
Ipecac	Cephalaeis ipecacuanha	Emetine	Relief of amebic dysentery, abscess
Mandrake	Mandragora officinarum	Hyoscine	Hypnotic, antiemetic
Opium poppy	Papaver somniferum	Morphine, codeine, papaverine	Severe pain relief, muscle relaxation
Senna	Cassia senna	Anthraquinone	Purgative
Storax	Styrax benzoin	Benzoin	Relief of pressure sores
Strophanthus	Strophanthus gratus, or S. sarmentosus	Strophanthin	Heart stimulant
Thorn apple	Datura stramonium	Hyoscine	Hypnotic, antiemetic
Valerian	Valeriana officinalis	Valerian	Sedative
Willow	Salix species	Salicilin	Pain relief
Yellow bark	Cinchona calisaya	Quinine	Antimalaria

▲ ▶ Morphine is made from an extract of opium poppies (above). Belladonna (right) yields atropine, a sedative. Foxgloves (far right) are the source of digitalis, a powerful heart stimulant. The thorn apple (top right) produces hyoscine, used to stop vomiting.

that of salicylic acid (from the bark of the American black birch tree). The active ingredient of fox-gloves was found to be digitalis, belladonna contains the sedative atropine, and the species of poppy that was used medicinally yields opium (used in the form of a drug called laudanum). Morphine and codeine come from opium, as does diamorphine—better known as heroin.

In tropical South America the bark of cinchona trees was found to be effective against malaria. Its active ingredient was quinine. A weak dilution of quinine was used in "Indian tonic water"—a drink originally for medicinal use.

Manufacturing Medicines

During the 1880s and 1890s chemists worked hard to develop a medicine based on salicilin and salicylic acid. By 1899 the German company Friedrich Bayer was marketing a drug called "aspirin," a name derived from *acetylierte Spirsäure*, the German name for the chemical acetylated spiraeic acid that we now call acetylsalicylic acid.

In 1944 two chemists, Robert Burns Woodward and William von Eggers Doering, synthesized quinine, starting from simple ingredients. Professor Woodward later made strychnine (1949), cortisone (1951), and, in 1954, lysergic acid, the basis of LSD.

This established the trend that continues. Remedies contained in plants are identified, isolated, and then they, or compounds with a similar action, are manufactured from simple raw materials. At the same time, the search for plants with medicinal potential has intensified. Modern laboratory equipment can analyze substances and screen compounds for their likely effects cheaply and rapidly. Techniques of genetic engineering present an alternative way to produce medicines. Genes that direct cells to manufacture useful substances can be introduced into plants that are then cultivated.

Medicines must be used care-fully, because at certain doses they become poisonous. Plants make "medicinal" substances to deter predators: the substances are very potent poisons. Eating a single leaf of some plants, such as olean-der or foxglove, can prove fatal.

See Also | COMPETITION AND PLANT DEFENSES **4** 28 | POTATO FAMILY **10** 40 👁

Timber

TREES GROW BY ADDING LAYERS OF NEW CELLS around their trunks and branches just beneath the bark. Specialized cells are attached end to end to form channels through which water and mineral nutrients travel from the roots, and sugars travel from the leaves to all parts of the plant.

The walls of the living cells of trees contain lignin, a substance that makes them rigid. It also thickens the cell walls, eventually blocking the flow of liquid through them. The old cells also accumulate waste products from the living cells.

The tissue made from the hard, dead cells is known as the heartwood. It occupies the center of the trunk and branches, and strengthens them. It is because of this strong "backbone" that a tree is able to grow tall without falling over under its own weight. Outside the heartwood is the layer of living cells, called the sapwood, protected by a waterproof layer of dead cork cells. The cork is hard, and its rough exterior is the bark of the tree.

Trees into Timber

If the tree has been grown for timber, every part of the wood is used. The bark is stripped away and made into chips, which are used as fuel or sold to gardeners to spread on the ground to suppress weeds. Stripped of its bark, the outer, curved layers of the trunk are removed. Together with wood from the smaller branches

▲ Tree bark is used as fuel and for compost. Beneath it the curved wood is made into plywood. Thin planks are cut from below that, and thicker planks are cut from the center.

TIMBER TREES

	Common name	Scientific name	Principal uses
SOFTWOOD	Cedar of Lebanon	*Cedrus libani*	Furniture; joinery
	Cigar box cedar	*Cedrus odorata*	Joinery; cigar boxes
	Douglas fir	*Pseudotsuga mensiesii*	Building; joinery
	Grand fir	*Abies grandis*	Building; joinery; musical instruments
	Kauri pine	*Agathis robusta*	Joinery; plywood
	Larch	*Larix decidua*	Exterior building; poles; posts
	Norway spruce	*Picea abies*	Building; joinery; plywood; pulp
	Red fir	*Abies magnifica*	Building; joinery; musical instruments
	Sitka spruce	*Picea sitchensis*	Building; joinery; pulp; plywood
	Western hemlock	*Tsuga heterophylla*	Building; joinery
HARDWOOD	African mahogany	*Khaya senegalensis*	Furniture; joinery; veneer
	American ash	*Fraxinus americana*	Tool handles; sports goods; furniture
	American beech	*Fagus grandifolia*	Furniture; tool handles; floors
	Balsa	*Ochroma pyramidale*	Insulation; buoyancy; models
	Balsam poplar	*Populus balsamifera*	Matches; baskets; toys
	Brazilian rosewood	*Dalbergia nigra*	Furniture; veneer; musical instruments
	Ebony	*Diospyros ebenum*	Inlay; musical instruments
	English oak	*Quercus robur*	Furniture; joinery; veneers
	European ash	*Fraxinus excelsior*	Tool handles; sports goods; furniture
	Karri gum	*Eucalyptus diversicolor*	Heavy construction; beams; rafters
	Teak	*Tectona grandis*	Furniture; joinery; shipbuilding

they are made into chips that are used to make plywood. The trunk, now square in cross-section, is cut into lengths. Planks are taken from the outside, where the wood is usually free of knots. Knots occur near the center of the trunk. They weaken the wood and make it difficult to work. The center of the trunk is cut into thicker planks and thick beams.

Before it can be used, however, the timber must be seasoned. Seasoning dries the wood and is necessary because all wood retains a large amount of water. The beams and planks are stacked outdoors in layers under a water-proof roof, with space between them to allow air to circulate. After some months the stack is moved into a building where hot air is blown around it in a process called kilning. It takes 6–18 months to season timber outdoors and about one week to season it by kilning. It can be seasoned in about 12 hours by kilning in a sealed building that has had most of the air pumped out.

Uses of Timber

Most timber is sold to builders, who use it for items such as frames for roofs, beams and

▶ Harvested trunks, stripped of their branches, are often dropped into a river. The river carries them to the sawmill.

See Also | CELL TYPES AND TISSUES **1** 18 | STEMS **1** 28 | WATER AND WATER UPTAKE **3** 24 👁

rafters, floors, doors, and window frames in houses. Some houses are made entirely from wood, of course.

Better-quality wood will be used for furniture making, or joinery. The very best and most expensive wood will be cut into very thin sheets, known as veneer, which is glued to the exterior surfaces of furniture and then highly polished. The veneer gives the appearance of expensive, attractive, and solid wood. The rest of the wood will be made into a variety of other useful items, from handles for tools to telephone poles and fences.

Large amounts of timber are smashed to individual fibers and mixed with water to make a pulp. It is sprayed evenly onto mesh cylinders, peeled off, pressed, and dried. It is then mixed with substances to strengthen and whiten it to make paper.

Hardwood and Softwood

Different trees produce wood with different characteristics. Wood is classified as softwood or hardwood. Softwoods are produced by conifer trees, such as cedar, pine, hemlock, larch, and spruce. Such trees have leaves that are needles or small scales. Trees with broad leaves, such as oak, ash, beech, ebony, and teak, produce hardwood. Despite the names, not all softwoods are softer than all hardwoods. Balsa is classed as a hardwood but is very light, and Douglas fir, a softwood, is fairly hard.

▶ Dipterocarp trees yield light timber that absorbs preservatives well. It is used for railroad ties and heavy construction, but the trees are harvested from natural forest faster than they can regrow. They are being stripped of their bark in Sabah, Malaysia.

It is the density of the wood that makes the difference. Lignum vitae is the hardest of all woods because it is densest: one cubic foot weighs 80 pounds (1.25 tonnes per cubic meter). The density of Douglas fir is about 32 pounds per cubic foot (497 kg per cubic meter). Balsa averages about 8 pounds per cubic foot (128 kg per cubic meter).

Wood from the Sitka spruce is used to make paper. Norway spruce wood is used in building and to make boxes. The best boxes are made with boxwood: it is so hard it can be carved with great detail. Lignum vitae is made into bowling balls, mallet heads, and pulleys, and used as the bushing (lining) of the stern tubes of the propeller shafts of ships. Its name is Latin for wood of life because the wood and resin from it were once used medicinally.

Fences, gates, and boats are often made from larch. Scotch pine is used to make paper, boxes, railroad ties, and telephone poles. Pencils are made from the red or pencil cedar (which is a juniper).

PROTECTING OUR WORLD

CONSERVING FORESTS

Between 1981 and 1990 the area covered by tropical forests shrank by 0.7 percent in Africa, 1.2 percent in Asia and the Pacific islands, and 0.8 percent in the Caribbean islands and South America. Some loss is due to logging, but the main cause has been forest clearance for farmland. Plantations are being set up in tropical countries. In the future they will supply timber, allowing some of the natural forest to remain undisturbed.

In temperate countries timber comes from managed natural forest or plantations. The total area of forest is increasing. U.S. forests decrease in area by 740,000 acres (300,000 hectares) a year. European forests increase by 494,000 acres (200,000 hectares) a year. Russian forests increase by 4.9 million acres (2 million hectares) a year.

Forest Conservation

Tropical timbers include some of the hardest and most attractive woods, such as ebony, mahogany, and teak. They are usually taken from the natural forest, where felling individual trees often damages many more. Increasingly, instead of this logging method, trees are being grown and felled in sustainable plantations instead.

Temperate species used to be harvested in the forest, too. Tree plantations for timber were first planted in Britain in the 17th century. In North America and Russia there is more natural forest. The forests are conserved by restricting the amount of timber that can be taken, allowing time for the trees to regenerate.

▼ **Plantations provide an alternative to harvesting primary forest.**

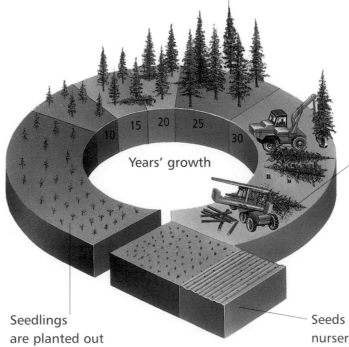

Weaker trees are felled to give more light and nutrients to the others

After the mature trees are felled, the branches are stripped and the trunks sawn into logs to enable transportation to the processing plant

Years' growth

Seedlings are planted out in the forest

Seeds are planted in a nursery where they grow to seedlings

See Also | PLANTS UNDER THREAT **4** 44 | WHAT IS A CONIFER **8** 4 | OAK AND BEECH FAMILY **10** 12 👁

Plants in Horticulture

AS WELL AS SUPPLYING US WITH FOOD, FIBER, AND TIMBER, plants also delight our senses. Many are highly ornamental and are grown for their flowers—sometimes perfumed—or foliage. They decorate public parks and private gardens, where plants are chosen because of their attractive appearance. They also decorate our homes, as indoor plants growing in pots or as cut flowers.

Flower-sellers had stalls in the markets of ancient Athens, and by the 1st century A.D. the cultivation of flowers had become a substantial industry in Rome. It was fashionable to add flowers to food: violets were mixed with salads to provide color, and dessert might be stewed roses.

Gardens were cherished in ancient Egypt, and Babylon (now Iraq) was the site of the Hanging Gardens, one of the wonders of the ancient world. North of Babylon lay the site of the Garden of Eden. Flower gardens were popular throughout the Middle East; and when Islam spread, first into Persia (now Iran), then to Spain, and finally to India, Muslims took with them a love of gardens and their favorite plants.

Roses

Roses were cultivated in ancient Greece, and the Romans may have carried the dog rose to northern Europe, where it now grows wild. The advance of Islam brought many new varieties to Western Europe. There are about 100 species of roses, only a few of which have been domesticated. They have been crossbred over such a long period that there are now many thousands of varieties.

The French rose from southwestern Europe is an original species of rose. It was cultivated in the 12th century A.D. The shrub grows about 4 feet (1.2 m) tall and has pink or crimson flowers. The musk rose from the Himalayas, a tall shrub with white flowers, was grown across Europe by the end of the 16th century. The crossing of the French and musk roses produced the damask rose.

Tulips

Roses are not the only garden favorite we owe to Islam. Multi-colored tulips were in Iran in the 13th century. Tulip cultivation spread from Iran to Turkey, and in the 16th century tulip bulbs were imported into Europe. They became so sought-after that in 1634 "tulipomania" was triggered in the Netherlands, with people paying huge sums for a single

---

PROTECTING OUR WORLD

SAVING WILD FLOWERS

Wild flowers are so popular that gathering wild plants to sell is big business. Sometimes the bulbs or corms of rare plants are exported and offered for sale in garden stores. This had led to a decline in the number of flowering plants in the wild because, even if the roots of the plant are left in the ground, removing the flower prevents the plants from producing seed. Most wild plants are now protected. They will remain safe only if customers always check the origin of what they buy, ensuring items are not taken from the wild.

bulb. The frenzy ended in 1637, but tulips remained popular.

Crocuses and daffodils followed this migration from southeast to northwest, and as flower gardening became more widespread, many other plants were domesticated.

Gardening As an Industry

As industrialization spread in the late 19th and early 20th centuries, increasing numbers of people moved to cities. As their prosperity rose, so did their demand for cut flowers, indoor houseplants, and plants to cultivate in their own small gardens.

A major industry developed to supply this market. In the United States people annually spend an average 0.2 percent of their income on flowers. Growers of cut flowers compete intensely to be first to market. Suburban centers selling to amateur gardeners are large and usually crowded.

Sustaining such operations there are nurseries and experimental stations where new varieties are developed. It takes many years to create a distinctive new variety of a popular flower, but the breeder who succeeds can earn a great deal of money from it.

▶ Experimental plants grow in large, colorful plots. Breeding plants for sale as plants, cut flowers, or seeds is big business.

See Also | *LILY FAMILY* **9** *20* | *DAFFODIL FAMILY* **9** *24* | *ROSE FAMILY* **10** *26* 👁

Glossary

alcohol An organic (carbon-containing) substance in which one hydrogen atom in the molecule is replaced by a hydroxyl group (–OH). The names of alcohols end in "ol." YEAST FERMENTATION of SUGAR produces the alcohol ethanol, the alcohol present in alcoholic drinks.

anthocyanins A group of red, blue, or violet pigments that are found in the cells of flowers, stems, leaves, and fruits.

aril A fleshy outer covering to a seed. The fleshy cup surrounding the seed of a yew tree is an aril, and the arils surrounding nutmegs are dried to produce the spice called mace.

berry A fleshy fruit that contains many seeds, but that does not open to release them. Most berries have a tough outer skin. Tomatoes and bell peppers are berries. Bananas are berries that have been modified by cultivation so that they no longer contain any seeds.

boll The ball of fibers that contains the seed of the cotton plant.

bread wheat A HEXAPLOID SPECIES of cultivated wheat that produces grains rich in GLUTEN.

bulbil A small bulb that grows from a bulb that develops above ground. A bulbil is easily detached, and a new plant can be grown from it. "Cloves" of garlic are bulbils.

bulgur wheat Whole wheat grains that have been boiled, dried, and crushed. It is made in North Africa and western Asia, but is now also popular in Europe and America.

carotenoid Any of a group of red, orange, and yellow pigments that are found in yellow or orange leaves and fruit and in the edible TAPROOT of the carrot. It is carotene that gives ripe tomatoes their red color. When we digest carotene, it is converted to vitamin A.

club wheat A widely grown HEXAPLOID SPECIES of cultivated wheat that produces its grains in a broad, short, club-shaped ear.

coir The name for the fibers obtained by combing out the thick layer of husk beneath the outer skin of a coconut. Coir is used to make ropes and coconut matting.

copra The white "meat" of a coconut after it has been dried and pressed. Copra is pressed to obtain coconut oil, used to make soap, for cooking, and in margarine. The residue left after pressing is made into a cake that is fed to farm livestock. Copra is the most valuable coconut product: good copra contains 60–65 percent oil.

cork The protective layer of dead, waterproof cells that forms the outer layer of the trunk and branches of a tree.

couscous A North African dish made from SEMOLINA that is cooked and mixed with water and oil.

cycad A cone-bearing plant of the phylum Cycadophyta. Male and female cones are borne on separate plants. Although they resemble palms, cycads are not related to them. They are GYMNOSPERMS and evolved millions of years earlier than palm trees.

diploid Having two copies of each chromosome in every cell.

domestication The process of transforming a SPECIES of wild plants, or animals, into a species that can be raised on farms. It involves altering the species so that it produces a greater quantity of more nutritious food than its wild ancestor.

durum A TETRAPLOID SPECIES of cultivated wheat that produces grains with more GLUTEN than any other species. It is used to make SEMOLINA and pasta.

einkorn A wild wheat, one of the DIPLOID SPECIES from which cultivated wheats have been derived.

emmer A TETRAPLOID SPECIES of wheat that was one of the first domesticated varieties. It is still grown in some places.

fermentation Form of respiration under conditions of oxygen shortage that results in the production of alcohol and carbon dioxide. Fermentation by converting glucose (a SUGAR) into ethanol (an ALCOHOL) is the process used to brew beer and make wine. Carbon dioxide released during fermentation in dough is trapped as bubbles. It is what makes the dough rise and the bread light.

genetic modification (also known as genetic engineering) The deliberate and controlled alteration of certain characteristics of an organism, or the introduction of new or altered characteristics to the organism, in order to improve it for agricultural or other use. The concept is based on traditional plant and animal breeding, in which only individuals possessing desired qualities were permitted to breed. While still controversial, this method is more precise, however, producing results more quickly, and it allows characteristics to be transferred between unrelated SPECIES. Crop plants have been bred to repel insect attack, to tolerate certain herbicides (resulting in major reduction in pesticide use), and to grow in soil that is too salty for most plants. Crops with improved nutritional quality are currently being developed. Plants are also being developed to produce medicines and industrial chemicals.

ginning The process of separating the seed from the lint of a cotton BOLL, prior to spinning and weaving, to make cotton cloth.

gluten A protein that is contained in wheat grains. It is elastic when wet and imparts a springy texture to bread dough.

gram One of a number of SPECIES of small beans, including the adzuki bean and mung bean, that can be used to produce beansprouts. The name "gram" comes originally from the Latin *granum*, meaning "grain," and refers to their small size.

gymnosperm A plant that does not produce true flowers and bears seeds that are not contained inside an ovary. At one time all seed-bearing plants were gymnosperms, but from about 100 million years ago they were largely replaced by flowering plants. The gymnosperms include coniferous plants, such as larch, pine, fir, and juniper, and CYCADS.

haploid Having only one copy of each chromosome in every cell.

hard wheat Wheat that produces grains rich in GLUTEN. It is used to make bread and pasta.

hardwood Wood from a broad-leaved tree, such as oak, beech, or ash.

heartwood The hard, dead tissue at the center of a tree trunk.

hexaploid Having six copies of each chromosome in every cell.

lignin A carbohydrate that is formed in the cell walls of many plants, but especially woody plants. It stiffens the cell walls by linking fibers together.

linseed oil An oil that is obtained by crushing the seeds of the flax plant. It dries and hardens on exposure to air and is used in the manufacture of paints, varnishes, and printing inks. Flax plants grown for oil have shorter stems and produce more seeds than the varieties grown for fiber.

lint The fibers of a cotton BOLL after they have been dried by exposing them to the air. (A fine material made from linen and used for dressing wounds is also called lint.)

malt Barley grains that are allowed to sprout and are then dried slowly.

maltose A SUGAR that is formed when STARCH is broken down rapidly in a sprouting seed.

mealies The name by which corn (maize) is known in much of Africa.

millet Several SPECIES of cultivated grasses that produce small grains. They are usually prepared for eating by being ground or pounded and then made into a porridge.

paddy A field that is flooded to a depth of a few inches in order to grow rice, which is planted as seedlings in the mud. The field is later drained so that the ground is dry for harvesting.

palm oil An edible oil that is also used in soap-making. It is obtained from the fruit of the oil palm, a tree that yields more oil per acre of land than any other source of vegetable oil or animal fat.

photosynthesis The process by which green plants manufacture SUGAR from carbon dioxide and water, using sunlight energy.

physic garden A garden in which medicinal herbs are grown. Physic is an old word for medicine.

pulses Edible seeds such as beans, lentils, and chickpeas (also called Bengal GRAM) that are cooked until they resemble porridge. Their name comes from *puls*, Latin for porridge.

retting The process of stiffening and loosening the outer part of the stems of flax plants by prolonged soaking in water followed by drying. The stems may be immersed in a pond or laid on damp grass (dew retting). Retting partly decomposes the stem, leaving it brittle.

sago A form of STARCH that is obtained from the pith beneath the bark of several plants, the most important being the sago palm. After a tree is felled, the bark is removed, and the pith scooped out. It is then washed and either dried to make sago flour or pressed through a sieve onto a hot surface to make pearl sago.

sapwood The living tissue that lies just beneath the bark of a tree.

semolina Coarsely ground wheat grains.

soft wheat Wheat that produces grains containing only small amounts of GLUTEN. It is used to make cakes and pastries.

softwood Wood from a coniferous tree, such as pine, hemlock, fir, or spruce.

species A group of organisms that can breed among themselves but not with other organisms.

spelt One of the earliest SPECIES of cultivated wheat. It is difficult to

THRESH and nowadays is grown only on a small scale. It is HEXAPLOID.

starch The principal form in which plants store nutrients. It is made during PHOTOSYNTHESIS. Starch is readily converted to sugars by enzymes known as amylases. Potato TUBERS, cassava roots, and cereal grains are among the plant organs in which starch is stored.

stigma The part of a flower that captures pollen and on which the pollen grain starts to grow. It is located at the tip of the STYLE. In insect-pollinated flowers the stigma combs pollen from the bodies of insects.

style A stalklike structure that links the ovary of a flower with the STIGMA.

sugar A compound of carbon and hydrogen (a carbohydrate) that consists of simple units with the general formula $(CH_2O)n$; glucose and fructose are both $C_6H_{12}O_6$. Glucose is the principal energy food for all organisms and the molecular unit from which STARCH, cellulose, and several other carbohydrates are made.

taproot The primary root of a plant derived from the radicle of the embryo, forming a stout tapering root that grows vertically downward. Some plants have swollen taproots in which nutrients are stored. Carrots and parsnips are edible taproots.

teosinte A wild relative of corn (maize) that is one of the SPECIES from which varieties of cultivated corn were derived.

tetraploid Having four copies of each chromosome in every cell.

threshing The process of mechanically separating the grain from the ear of a cereal plant, either by beating the plant with a jointed stick, called a flail, or by machine.

tuber A swollen section of a stem or root in which nutrients are stored and that lasts for only one year. Root tubers, such as those of the dahlia, develop from adventitious roots (roots that grow in unusual positions). Stem tubers, such as those of the potato, possess buds, called "eyes," from which new stems grow.

veneer A very thin sheet that is cut from a piece of valuable, attractive wood and glued to the outer surface of an article made from a cheaper wood in order to improve the appearance of the article.

yeast One of a number of SPECIES of single-celled fungi that obtain the energy they need by converting glucose (a SUGAR) into ethanol (an ALCOHOL) and carbon dioxide.

Scientific Names

In this set common names have been used wherever possible. Listed below are the plants mentioned in this volume for which scientific names have not already been given. See Volume 1, page 7 for further detail on the naming of plants.

adzuki bean *Vigna angularis*
akee *Blighia sapida*
allspice *Pimenta dioica*
almond *Prunus amygdalus, P. dulcis*
American black birch *Betula lenta*
American plum *Prunus americana*
apple *Malus* species
apricot *Prunus armeniaca*
arrowroot *Maranta arundinacea*
asparagus *Asparagus officinalis*
avocado *Persea americana*
balsa *Ochroma pyramidale*
bamboos *Bambusa* species
banana *Musa acuminata*
barley (six-rowed) *Hordeum vulgare*
barley (two-rowed) *Hordeum distichon*
basil *Ocimum basilicum*
beeches *Fagus* species
beetroot *Beta vulgaris*
belladonna *Atropa belladonna*

bell or sweet pepper *Capsicum annuum*
black maple *Acer nigrum*
black pepper *Piper nigrum*
black walnut *Juglans nigra*
box *Buxus sempervirens*
Brazil nut *Bertholletia excelsa*
bread wheat *Triticum aestivum*
breadfruit *Artocarpus altilis*
broad bean *Vicia faba*
Brussels sprouts *Brassica oleracea* var. *gemmifera*
butter bean *Phaseolus lunatus*
butternut *Juglans cinerea*
cabbage palm *Oreodoxa oleracea*
calabrese *Brassica oleracea* var. *italica*
cantaloupe *Cucumis melo* var. *cantalupensis*
capsicum *Capsicum anuum*
caraway *Carum carvi*
cardamom *Elettaria cardamomum*
cardoon *Cynara cardunculus*

carrot *Daucus carota sativus*
cashew nut *Anacardium occidentale*
cassava *Manihot utilissima*
cauliflower *Brassica oleracea* var. *botrytis*
cedar *Cedrus libani*
celeriac *Apium graveolens* var. *rapaceum*
celery *Apium graveolens*
chamomile *Chamaemelum nobile*
cherry plum *Prunus cerasifera*
chervil *Anthriscus cerefolium*
chickpea *Cicer arietinum*
chicory *Cichorium intybus*
chili *Capsicum annuum*
Chinese water chestnut *Eleocharis tuberosa*
cinchona *Cinchona micrantha*
cinnamon *Cinnamomum zeylanicum*
cloves *Syzygium aromaticum*
club wheat *Triticum compactum*
cocoa *Theobroma cacao*
coconut palm *Cocos nucifera*

coffee *Coffea arabica, C. canephora, C. liberica*
coriander *Coriandrum sativum*
corn (maize) *Zea mays*
cotton *Gossypium* species
crocuses *Crocus* species
cucumber *Cucumis sativus*
cumin *Cuminum cyminum*
curled kale *Brassica oleracea* var. *acephala*
daffodils *Narcissus* species
damask rose *Rosa damascena*
damson *Prunus institia*
dill *Anethum graveolens*
dog rose *Rosa canina*
Douglas fir *Pseudotsuga mensiesii*
durian *Durio zibethinus*
durum wheat *Triticum durum*
ebony *Diospyros ebenum*
eggplant *Solanum melongena*
einkorn wheat *Triticum monococcum*
emmer wheat *Triticum dicoccum*
endive *Cichorium endiva*
esparto grass *Stipa tenacissima*
fennel *Foeniculum vulgare*
feverfew *Tanacetum parthenium*
flax *Linum usitatissimum*
foxglove *Digitalis purpurea, D. lanata*
foxtail millet *Setaria italica*
French bean *Phaseolus vulgaris*
French rose *Rosa gallica*
garden pea *Pisum sativum*
garlic *Allium sativum*
gherkin *Cucumis anguria*
ginger *Zingiber officinale*
grams *Vigna* species
grape vine *Vitis vinifera*
grapefruit *Citrus paradisi*
groundnut *Arachis hypogaea*
hard wheat *Triticum durum*
haricot bean *Phaseolus vulgaris*
hemlocks *Tsuga* species
hemp *Cannabis sativa*
hemp dogbane *Apocynum venetum*
honeydew melon *Cucumis melo* var. *saccharinus*
hops *Humulus lupulus*
Indian hemp *Apocynum cannabinum*
jack fruit *Artocarpus heterophyllus*
Japanese plum *Prunus triflora*
Jerusalem artichoke *Helianthus tuberosus*
jute *Corchorus* species
kale *Brassica oleracea* var. *medullosa*
kidney bean *Phaseolus vulgaris*
kohlrabi *Brassica oleracea* var. *gongylodes*
leek *Allium porrum*
lemon balm *Melissa officinalis*
lentil *Lens culinaris*
lettuce *Lactuca sativa*

lignum vitae *Guaiacum officinale*
lime *Citrus aurantifolia*
linseed *Linum usitatissimum*
litchi *Litchi chinensis*
loquat *Eriobotrya japonica*
mahogany (African) *Khaya senegalensis*
mango *Mangifera indica*
marrow *Cucurbita pepo*
melon *Cucumis melo*
mung bean *Vigna radiata*
musk rose *Rosa moschata*
myrrh *Myrrhis odorata*
nectarine *Prunus persica* var. *nectarina*
netted melon *Cucumis melo* var. *reticulatus*
Norway spruce *Picea abies*
nutmeg *Myristica fragrans*
nypa palm *Nypa fruticans*
oaks *Quercus* species
oats *Avena sativa*
oca *Oxalis tuberosa*
oleander *Nerium oleander*
olive *Olea europaea*
onion *Allium cepa*
oregano *Origanum vulgare*
palmyra palm *Borassus flabellifer*
parsley *Petroselinum crispum*
parsnip *Pastinaca sativa*
peach *Prunus persica*
peanut *Arachis hypogaea*
pea *Pisum sativum*
pear *Pyrus communis*
pecan *Carya illinoinensis*
pepper, black and white *Piper nigrum*
persimmon *Diospyros kaki*
pines *Pinus* species
pineapple *Ananas comosus*
pistachio *Pistacia vera*
plum *Prunus domestica*
pomelo *Citrus grandis*
poppies *Argemone glauca, Glaucium flavum*
poppy, opium *Papaver somniferum*
potato *Solanum tuberosum*
pumpkin *Cucurbita moschata*
rape *Brassica napus*
red cabbage *Brassica oleracea* vars. *bullata, capitata, sabauda*
red cedar *Juniperus virginiana*
rhubarb *Rheum rhabarbarum*
rice *Oryza* species
rosemary *Rosmarinus officinalis*
roses *Rosa* species
round cabbage *Brassica oleracea* var. *capitata*
runner bean *Phaseolus coccineus*
rye *Secale cereale*
safflower *Carthamus tinctorius*
saffron *Crocus sativus*

sage *Salvia officinalis*
sago palm *Metroxylon rumphii, M. sagu*
samphire *Crithmum maritimum*
savory *Satureja hortensis*
savoy cabbage *Brassica oleracea* vars. *capitata, bullata, sabauda*
scarlet runner bean *Phaseolus coccineus*
sea kale *Crambe maritima*
sesame *Sesamum indicum*
shallot *Allium cepa* var. *aggregatum*
Sitka spruce *Picea sitchensis*
sloe *Prunus spinosa*
sorghum *Sorghum vulgare*
soybean, soya *Glycine max*
spelt wheat *Triticum spelta*
spinach beet *Beta vulgaris cicla*
spruces *Picea* species
squashes *Cucurbita pepo*
strawberry *Fragaria ananassa*
sugar beet *Beta vulgaris*
sugar cane *Saccharum officinarum*
sugar maple *Acer saccharum*
sugar palm *Arenga pinnata*
sunflower *Helianthus annuus*
sweet chestnut *Castanea sativa*
sweet marjoram *Origanum majorana*
sweet orange *Citrus sinensis*
sweet potato *Ipomoea batatas*
tangerine *Citrus reticulata*
tansy *Tanacetum vulgare*
taro *Colocasia esculenta*
tarragon *Artemisia dracunculus*
tea *Camellia sinensis*
teak *Tectona grandis*
teosinte *Zea mays parviglumis*
tepary bean *Phaseolus acutifolius*
thorn apple *Datura stramonium*
thyme *Thymus vulgaris*
tomato *Lycopersicon esculentum*
tulips *Tulipa* species
turmeric *Curcuma domestica*
turnip *Brassica rapa*
ulluco *Ullucus tuberosus*
vanilla *Vanilla planifolia*
violets *Viola* species
walnut *Juglans regia*
water chestnut *Trapa natans*
watermelon *Citrullus lanatus*
wheat *Triticum* species
wild cabbage *Brassica oleracea*
wild date palm *Phoenix sylvestris*
wild einkorn wheat *Triticum boeoticum*
wild emmer wheat *Triticum dicoccoides*
wild goat grass *Aegilops speltoides, A. squarrosa*
willows *Salix* species
yams *Dioscorea* species
yam bean *Pachyrrhizus erosus*

Set Index

Major entries are shown by bold key words with relevant page numbers underlined.
Bold numbers indicate volumes.
Italic numbers indicate picture captions.

Scientific names of plants cited under common names in this Index are to be found at the end of each individual volume.

A

abacá *see* hemp
Abies **8**: <u>18–21</u>
abscisic acid **3**: *13*, 14–16
abscission **3**: *13, 17*
acacia **2**: 9, 12, **10**: 30, 32
achene **2**: *35*, **9**: 46, **10**: 10
acid rain **8**: 17, *17*
aconite **10**: 8
  winter **10**: *9*, 10
acorn **2**: 32, 39, **10**: 12, *13*
actinomorphic **2**: *4*
active transport **3**: 33
adder's-tongue spearwort **10**: 10
adenosine triphosphate (ATP) **3**: 11, 31–32
adhesion **3**: *26*, 27–28
Aechmea nudicaulis **9**: *35*
Agapetes macrantha **10**: *23*
agar **6**: 21
agaric **6**: *34, 37*, 41
  fly **6**: *30, 36*
agave **5**: 41
Agent Orange **3**: 12
aging **3**: 16, *17*
Aglaophyton **7**: 18, *18*
agrimony **2**: 39
air plant *see* epiphyte
akee **5**: *10*, 11
albardine **5**: 35
alcohol **5**: 41, *41*, **6**: 44
alder **2**: 24, **4**: 24
aleurone layer **1**: 45, *45*, **2**: *33*, **3**: 14
alexanders **5**: 37
alfalfa **2**: 12, 20, **3**: 34–35, **4**: 17, 23, **10**: 30
algae **1**: 12, **3**: 33, 49, **6**: *9*, <u>14–29</u>, *14–29*, **7**: 9
  blue-green *see* cyanobacteria
  brown 6: <u>26–28</u>, *26–28*
  carotenoids **3**: 9
  chloroplast **1**: 12
  conjugating green **6**: 24, *24*
  coralline (stony red) **6**: 20–21, *20*
  evolution **1**: 5, **6**: *4*, 5, 14, 22
  green 1: *15*, **6**: <u>22–25</u>, *22–25*, 48
  lichens **6**: 48–49
  multicellular **6**: 24–25
  photosynthesis **3**: 5, **6**: 26
  red 6: <u>20–21</u>, *20, 21*
  siphonous **6**: 24
  symbiosis **6**: 22
  see also diatom; dinoflagellate; seaweed; slime mold; water mold
alginic acid (algin) **6**: 26
Alismataceae 9: <u>46–47</u>
allele **2**: 42–45, *42, 43*
alley cropping **4**: 48

Allium **9**: *21*
allspice **5**: 36, 38
Alluaudia dumosa **4**: *32*
almond **5**: 14, *14*, 31, **10**: 28
aloe **9**: 21, *21*, 22
alpine snowbell **3**: 49
amaranthus **9**: 5
Amaryllidaceae 9: <u>24–27</u>
"amaryllis" **9**: *27*
ameba **6**: 14, 15, 17
amino acid **1**: 45, **3**: 10, 31, **10**: 30, 32
Anabaena **3**: 35, **4**: 17
anaphase **1**: 17, *17*, **2**: *40, 41, 41*
andiroba **5**: 31
Aneilema beninense **9**: 36
anemone **10**: 8, *9*, 10
angelica **5**: 37
angiosperm **1**: *5*, **4**: *4*, **6**: 11, **9**: 8
  see also flowering plants
angostura **5**: 38
anise **5**: *38*
annual **1**: *11*, **2**: 14, **3**: 16, **5**: 4
annulus **7**: 38, *39*
Anoectochilus roxburghii **9**: *19*
Antarctic *see* polar biome
anther **2**: *4, 6, 7, 7, 9, 26*, **6**: *11*, **9**: *4, 6, 7*
antheridial disk **7**: *6*
antheridium **6**: 10, *10*, 45, *45*, **7**: 6, *6, 10, 11*, 25, *25, 30*, 31, 39, *39*
antherozoid **7**: 10, *11*
anthocyanin **2**: 10, *10*
anthoxanthin **2**: 10
anu **5**: *27*
apache plume **2**: 36
Apiaceae 10: <u>38–39</u>
apical (terminal) bud **1**: *10*, 11, 28, *28, 34, 36*, **2**: 46, **3**: *14*, 15
apple **2**: 6, *33, 34*, 35, 49, **3**: 16, **5**: 8, *8*, 10, 41, **10**: 26, 28
  crab **10**: 28
apple scab **6**: *45*
apricot **5**: *8*, 10, **10**: 28
aquatic plants **1**: 21, 26, **2**: 25, *25*, **3**: 47–49, 48, 49, **9**: 16, 46, 48
  buoyancy **1**: *21*, **3**: 47–48, *48*, **6**: 28, **7**: 38
  carnivorous plants **3**: 39, *39*
  diatoms 6: 14, <u>18–19</u>, *18, 19*
  evolution **6**: 8
  free-floating **9**: 38, *39*, 48, *49*
  lake food web and food pyramid **4**: *9*
  leaves **1**: 41
  photosynthesis **3**: *5*

vegetative reproduction **2**: 48
  see also algae
aquifer **4**: 13
aquilegia *see* columbine
Araceae 9: <u>38–39</u>
Araucaria **8**: <u>38–39</u>
Arbor vitae **8**: <u>44–45</u>, *45*
  American (white cedar) **8**: 44–45, *45*
  Japanese **8**: 45, *45*
  Korean **8**: 44–45
  oriental **8**: 45
  Sichuan **8**: 45
  western red cedar **8**: 44, 45
archangel, yellow **10**: 42
archegoniophore **7**: *6*
archegonium **6**: 10, *10*, **7**: 6, *6, 10, 11*, 25, *25, 26, 26, 30*, 31, 39, *39*, 44
Arctic *see* polar biome
Arecaceae 9: <u>30–33</u>
areole **10**: 14, *15*
aril **2**: *38*, **5**: 36, **8**: *8*, 48, 49
Armillaria tabescens **6**: *36*
arrowhead **3**: 48, **9**: 46, *47*
arrowroot **5**: *27*, 28, 32, 33
artillery fungus **6**: 38
artist's conk **6**: 37
arum **2**: 12, 20, 21, **3**: 8, **9**: 5, 48
  family 9: <u>38–39</u>, *38, 39*, titan **2**: 15, 20
  wild **2**: *20*, 21
asafetida **10**: 38
ascocarp **6**: 44, 47
ascogonium **6**: 45, *45*
Ascomycota 6: 30, <u>44–47</u>, *44–47*, 48–49
ascospore **6**: 45
ascus **6**: 30, 44–47, *45*
asexual reproduction *see* vegetative reproduction
ash **5**: 46
  American **5**: 44
  European **5**: 44
  mountain **10**: 4
asparagus **5**: 19, *19*, **9**: 20
asparagus fern **9**: 20
aspen **4**: *4*
  quaking **4**: 30
aster **10**: 48
Asteraceae 10: <u>46–49</u>
Asteroxylon **7**: 18, 19
ATP *see* adenosine triphosphate
aubretia **10**: 20
auphorbia **1**: *43*
Australian floristic realm **4**: 35, *35*
autumn crocus **9**: 21, *21*
auxin **3**: 12–16, *13, 15, 16, 17*, 19–20
auxospore **6**: 19
avens **10**: 26, 28
  mountain **2**: 9, **3**: 49

wood **2**: 39
avocado **2**: 38, **5**: 10, 21, *22*
awn **9**: *13*
axil **1**: 10, *10*, 28, **9**: 30, 36
axis **9**: 39
azalea **10**: 22
Azotobacter **3**: 34, **4**: 17

B

babassú **5**: 31
bachelor's button **10**: 10
Bacillariophyta 6: <u>18–19</u>
bacteria **4**: 14, 18, **6**: *4, 5, 6*, <u>12–13</u>, *12*, **7**: 18, 19
  evolution **1**: *5*
  nitrogen-fixing **3**: 34–35, *34, 35*, **4**: 17
  photosynthesis **3**: 5, 35, **6**: 6, *6*, 12–13
  structure **6**: *12*
  see also cyanobacteria
bald cypress **1**: 27, **3**: 47, **8**: 37, *37*
balsa **5**: 44, 46
balsam **2**: 39
bamboo **1**: 33, **5**: *22*, 35, **9**: 12, *13*
banana **2**: 23, 34, **5**: *10*, **family 9**: <u>40–41</u>, *41*
banyan **1**: 26
baobab **1**: 32, **2**: 23
bark **1**: 30–31, *47*, 48–49, *49*, **5**: 44, 48, **8**: 8–9
  roots **1**: 26
barley **3**: *28*, **5**: 4, 6, 12, *12*, 41, **9**: 5
bases **1**: 16
Basidiomycota 6: 30, <u>34–43</u>, 37, 38–39, *39*, 48–49
basidiospore **6**: 35, 35
basidium **6**: 30, 35, *35*
basil **5**: 36, *37*, **10**: 42
basswood **4**: 39
bauhinia, red **10**: *31*
bay **5**: *38*
  sweet **10**: 7
beach grass **3**: 45
bean **1**: 44–45, **2**: 6, 29, 39, **3**: *24*, 34–35, **4**: 16, 31, **5**: 5, 16, 24–25, *24–25*
  broad **1**: *45*, **2**: *29*, **5**: 5, 25, *25*
  butter **5**: 25, *25*
  family 10: <u>30–33</u>
  French **5**: 25, *25*
  haricot **5**: 25, *25*
  kidney **5**: 5, 25, *25*
  mung **10**: 30
  runner **1**: *44*, **3**: *28*, **5**: 5, 25, *25*, **10**: 30
  tepary **5**: 5
bearberry **10**: 23
beech 1: 26, 40, **3**: *17*, **4**: *21*, 39, **5**: 46
  American **5**: 44

copper **3**: 8
  European **3**: 8, *9*, **9**: *22*
  family 10: <u>12–13</u>
  oriental **10**: *13*
  southern **10**: 12, *13*
beet **5**: 19, *27*
beetroot **5**: 19
begonia **1**: 43, *43*, **3**: 8, *8*
belladonna *see* deadly nightshade
bellflower
  Chilean **9**: *20*, 22
  family 10: <u>44–45</u>, *45*
bell pepper *see* pepper
ben **5**: 31
bent grass **4**: 23
Bermuda grass **9**: 15
berry **2**: 14, *34*, **10**: 36
  pepo **5**: 18
  see also fruit
betel nut **5**: *14*
beverages 5: <u>40–41</u>
biennial **3**: 16, 23, 42–44, *43*
big tree *see* redwood, giant
bilberry **5**: 8, **10**: 22
biogeography **4**: 26–27, *26, 27*, 34–35
bioluminescence **6**: 19
biomes 4: 8, <u>36–43</u>, *36–37*
  North American **4**: 43
birch **2**: 24, 25
  American black **5**: 42, 43
  dwarf **4**: 38
  paper **4**: 30
  silver **4**: 23
bird-of-paradise flower **2**: 13, 14, 24
bird-of-paradise shrub **10**: *31*
bird's nest fungus **6**: 38
  white-egg **6**: *39*
Biscutella didyma **10**: *21*
blackberry **2**: 34, *34*, 46, *46*, **5**: 8, **10**: 27, 28
blackthorn **10**: 26
bladderwort **3**: 39, *39*
blazing star **10**: *47*
blue grama **4**: 43
blue-eyed grass **9**: 28, 29
blue-green algae *see* cyanobacteria
bluebell **1**: *17*, **2**: *10*, **9**: *22*
  Scottish **10**: 44
blueberry **5**: 8, **10**: 22
bluebunch wheatgrass **4**: 43
bluestem grass **4**: 24, 43
blusher **6**: *36*
bok choy **5**: 20
bolete **6**: 37, *37*, 41
  bay **6**: *36*, 37
  devil's **6**: 37
  king **6**: 37
  slippery jack **6**: 41
borage **10**: *4*
boreal forest **4**: 36, 38
  see also conifer

Further Reading Volume 5: Plants Used by People

Medicinal Plants of the World by Ivan A. Ross. Humana Press, 1999

The Fruited Plain: The Story of American Agriculture by Walter Ebeling. University of California Press, 1979.

The Oxford Book of Food Plants by S.G. Harrison, G.B. Masefield, and Michael Wallis. Oxford University Press, 1969.

The Plant Book by D.J. Mabberley. Cambridge University Press, 1987.

Useful website addresses

Cyclamen mirabile
www.cyclamen.org/mirabile.htm

Evolution of Crop Plants
agronomy.ucdavis.edu/gepts/pb143.htm

Fiber Plants
www.scs.leeds.ac.uk/pfaf/fibplant.html

Food and Grain Legumes by F.J. Muehlbauer
www.hort.purdue.edu/newcrop/proceedings1993/v2-256.html

Geography of Agriculture by Matt Rosenberg
geography.about.com/edu.../aa022398.htm

A Guide to Medicinal and Aromatic Plants
www.hort.purdue.edu/newcrop/med-aro/default.html

Natural food-Grains Beans and Seeds
www.naturalhub.com/natural_food_guide_grains_beans_seeds.htm

Physicians, Fads, and Pharmaceuticals: A History of Aspirin by Anne Adina Judith Andermann.
www.mjm.mcgill.ca/issues/v02n02/aspirin.html

Plants for a Future: A Resource and Information Centre for Edible and Other Useful Plants
www.scs.leeds.ac.uk/pfaf/index.html

Royal Botanic Gardens, Kew
www.rbgkew.org/uk

Traditional Herbal & Plant Knowledge, Identifications
indy4.fdl.cc.mn.us/~isk/food/plants.html

Picture Credits Volume 5: Plants Used by People

Abbreviations
HS Holt Studios

All photographs are Andromeda Oxford Limited copyright except:

4 Ancient Art and Architecture Collection/R. Sheridan; 7 HS/Willem Harinck; **10** HS/Inga Spence; **13** Powerstock/Zefa Photo Library; **17** HS/Inga Spence; **24** HS/Willem Harinck; **30** G. Bateman; **33** Cyril Webster/A.N.T. Photo Library; **34** HS/Inga Spence; **40** HS/Nigel Cattlin; **41** Explorer/Hervy; **43tl and tr** HS/Nigel Cattlin; **43cl** HS/Mike Amphlett; **45** Robert Harding Picture Library; **47** Planet Earth Pictures/Richard Matthews

While every effort has been made to trace the copyright holders of illustrations reproduced in this book, the publishers will be pleased to rectify any omissions or inaccuracies.